C000182933

# ROWLEY REGIS

## A History

*A quiet scene on the Dudley no. 2 canal at Warren's Hall Park.*

# ROWLEY REGIS
## A History

Edward Chitham

Phillimore

2006

Published by
PHILLIMORE & CO. LTD
Shopwyke Manor Barn, Chichester, West Sussex, England
www.phillimore.co.uk

ISBN    1-86077-418-0
ISBN 13    978-1-86077-418-8

Printed and bound in Great Britain by
CAMBRIDGE PRINTING

# Contents

List of Illustrations . . . . . . . . . . . . . . . . . . . . . . . . . . . . . vii

Acknowledgements . . . . . . . . . . . . . . . . . . . . . . . . . . . . . .ix

I    Earliest Times . . . . . . . . . . . . . . . . . . . . . . . . . . . . . . . . . .1

II   Reconstructing Medieval Rowley . . . . . . . . . . . . . . . . . . . 9

III  Tudors and Stuarts . . . . . . . . . . . . . . . . . . . . . . . . . . .17

IV  The Eighteenth Century . . . . . . . . . . . . . . . . . . . . . . . . 28

V   Beginnings of the Industrial Revolution . . . . . . . . . . . . . . 39

VI  Administrative Collapse . . . . . . . . . . . . . . . . . . . . . . . . . . 47

VII  Heavy Industry . . . . . . . . . . . . . . . . . . . . . . . . . . . . . . . .51

VIII Quarrying and Brick Making . . . . . . . . . . . . . . . . . . . . . 63

IX  Nail and Chain Making . . . . . . . . . . . . . . . . . . . . . . . . .71

X   Transport in Rowley . . . . . . . . . . . . . . . . . . . . . . . . . . . 77

XI  Rowley Parish Church and the Church of England . . . . . . . 90

XII  Nonconformist Churches and Chapels . . . . . . . . . . . . . . . 97

XIII Education . . . . . . . . . . . . . . . . . . . . . . . . . . . . . . . . . . . .103

XIV Sports, Pastimes and Popular Culture . . . . . . . . . . . . . . . 111

XV  Strikes, Wars and Local Government . . . . . . . . . . . . . . . . .117

XVI Reorganisation and After . . . . . . . . . . . . . . . . . . . . . . . .122

Bibliography . . . . . . . . . . . . . . . . . . . . . . . . . . . . . . . . . . . 131

Index . . . . . . . . . . . . . . . . . . . . . . . . . . . . . . . . . . . . . . . . .133

# List of Illustrations

*Frontispiece:* The Dudley no. 2 canal at Warren's Hall Park

1 View from near Tippity Green.......1
2 Roman coins................... 2
3 Contour map of Rowley Regis......3
4 The Rowley Hailstone............ 4
5 Rowley in the 15th century.........5
6 Pieces of Rowley rag............ 6
7 Boundary brook at Grovelands......7
8 Plan of Camp Hawes............. 8
9 Farmhouse in Mincing Lane....... 9
10 The medieval church tower .......10
11 The stump of Haden Cross ....... 11
12 Notice board at Warren's Hall.....12
13 Moat Leasow at Warren's Hall.....12
14 Cottage at Warren's Hall..........13
15 Ruins of Halesowen Abbey........14
16 Rowley church before 1840........14
17 Tividale Hall...................15
18 Sir John Turton................17
19 Moor Lane ...................18
20 Stone buildings at Haden Hill......19
21 The old font of Rowley church....19
22 Oak House, West Bromwich....... 20
23 Plan of Brickhouse Farm..........21
24 Portway Hall...................22
25 Brades Hall Farm...............23
26 Rowley Hall foundations ........ 24
27 Portway Hall door.............. 24
28 Map of Rowley Somery ..........25
29 Haden Hill conservation notice.... 26
30 Haden Hill 'Tudor House' ........27
31 Portway farmhouse ..............28
32 Hailstone Farm................ 29
33 Site of Cradley Forge............ 30
34 Homestead at Oakham.......... 30
35 Cottages at Oakham .............31
36 Old houses in Carnegie Road ......31
37 Seventeenth-century church bell....32
38 A lane on Turner's Hill..........32
39 1663 house in Siviter's Lane .......33
40 Houses at Rowley Village .........33
41 James Woodhouse ...............34
42 Categories of nail................34
43 Dobbs Bank ...................35
44 Former Style House Farm .........35
45 Shops and houses, Rowley.........36
46 Blue Bell Farm, Old Hill..........36
47 The *Robert Peel*..................37
48 Stone cottage in Hawes Lane.......37
49 Plaque at Reddall Hill House......38
50 The Spring House (*Royal Oak*).....39
51 The Gaunt memorial............ 40
52 Club Buildings .................41
53 Row of houses, Blackheath........41
54 Corngreaves Hall ............... 42
55 Beauty Bank ...................43
56 George Barrs.................. 44
57 Graves at Rowley church ........ 44
58 St Luke's churchyard .............45
59 The *Barley Mow*, Tividale........ 46
60 Map of Rowley Village ........... 48
61 The Hailstone in 1845 ............ 49
62 'The Gin', by R. Chattock..........51
63 Timbertree Colliery...............52
64 Waterfall Lane pumping station ....53
65 Black Waggon pit.................53
66 Coalminers at work...............54

67 Turnpike tickets . . . . . . . . . . . . . . . . .54
68 The anchor for the *Titanic* . . . . . . . .55
69 The *Handel Hotel*, Blackheath . . . . . .55
70 The *Bull's Head*, Tippity Green . . . . .55
71 Plan of Rowley Hall . . . . . . . . . . . . .56
72 'Cobbs' engine house. . . . . . . . . . . . .57
73 Tividale aqueduct. . . . . . . . . . . . . . .57
74 Dudley Canal No. 2 . . . . . . . . . . . . . .58
75 The *Boat*, Old Hill. . . . . . . . . . . . . . .58
76 Canal bridge at Cobbs. . . . . . . . . . . .59
77 Canal scene at Station Road. . . . . . . 60
78 Netherton Canal tunnel entrance . . .61
79 The *Neptune*, Old Hill. . . . . . . . . . . .63
80 Brickyard 'pages'. . . . . . . . . . . . . . . . 64
81 Corngreaves Iron Works in 1885 . . . 64
82 Haden Hill House . . . . . . . . . . . . . . .65
83 Coal mines in Old Hill . . . . . . . . . . 66
84 Windmill End and Withymoor . . . . .67
85 Old quarry sites in Hawes Lane. . . . .67
86 Rowley stone quarry . . . . . . . . . . . . 68
87 Cottage at Perry's Lake . . . . . . . . . . 68
88 House at Perry's Lake . . . . . . . . . . . 69
89 The quarry stables . . . . . . . . . . . . . . 70
90 The nailer at work. . . . . . . . . . . . . . .72
91 Hayseech . . . . . . . . . . . . . . . . . . . . . .73
92 Mushroom Green chain-shop . . . . . .74
93 Half timbered wall built into
     19th-century cottage . . . . . . . . . . .75
94 A tram at Tividale . . . . . . . . . . . . . . .77
95 Cradley Heath tram. . . . . . . . . . . . . .78
96 Midland Red bus timetable . . . . . . .78
97 Plan of Old Hill station . . . . . . . . . .79
98 Bus tickets. . . . . . . . . . . . . . . . . . . . 80
99 Old Hill line train timetable . . . . . . 80
100 Running past Grovelands . . . . . . . . . .81
101 John's Lane bridge . . . . . . . . . . . . . . .82
102 Old mineral line, Warren's Hall. . . . .82
103 Thomas Lench letterhead . . . . . . . . .83
104 The end of Grovelands Farm. . . . . . .85
105 Shakespeare's works, Cox's Lane . . . .85
106 Doultons' works . . . . . . . . . . . . . . . . 86
107 Blackheath Market . . . . . . . . . . . . . . .87
108 Blackheath High Street . . . . . . . . . . .87
109 The day school, Rowley Village . . . .88
110 Waterfall Lane . . . . . . . . . . . . . . . . . .88
111 Handbill of hymns for 1845 . . . . . . . 89
112 Plan of St Luke's churchyard . . . . . . .91
113 St Luke's church . . . . . . . . . . . . . . . . .93
114 Knowle Methodist church . . . . . . . . .93
115 Rowley church after 1841. . . . . . . . . . 94
116 Rowley church after 1904 . . . . . . . . . .95
117 Foundation stone, Rowley church. . . 96
118 Providence Chapel, Mincing Lane . . .97
119 Christ Church, Cradley Heath . . . . . 98
120 Tividale Methodist Church. . . . . . . . 99
121 Organ recital at Grainger's Lane . . .100
122 Holy Trinity church . . . . . . . . . . . . .101
123 An aerial view of Tividale . . . . . . . .102
124 Reddal Hill school . . . . . . . . . . . . . .103
125 Rowley Endowed School . . . . . . . . .104
126 Log book, Wright's Lane school. . . .105
127 Part of an address by the
     Councillors Shakespeare . . . . . . . .105
128 Class at old grammar school . . . . . .106
129 View of new grammar school . . . . .106
130 The inside of the new school . . . . . .107
131 Macefields school . . . . . . . . . . . . . . .107
132 Mr G.T. Lloyd. . . . . . . . . . . . . . . . . .108
133 Corngreaves school . . . . . . . . . . . . .108
134 Wright's Lane school . . . . . . . . . . . .109
135 Rowley Borough coat of arms . . . . .109
136 'Noye's Fludde' at the school . . . . . .110
137 Old Hill Municipal Buildings . . . . . 112
138 Old Hill post office . . . . . . . . . . . . . 113
139 Pigeon food advertisement . . . . . . . 114
140 Plan of Britannia Park . . . . . . . . . . . 115
141 Reddal Hill library . . . . . . . . . . . . . .116
142 Rowley Regis Endowed School . . . . 119
143 Advertisements from 1923 . . . . . . . . .120
144 Advertisements from 1953 . . . . . . . . .121
145 Letterhead of Rowley Borough . . . . 122
146 Repetition Metalware advert . . . . . .123
147 Black Country Christmas card . . . . .123
148 Mary Macarthur Park, Lomey . . . . .124
149 Beeches Road pupils in 1956 . . . . . . 125
150 Warren's Hall Park . . . . . . . . . . . . . .126
151 Canal at Tividale . . . . . . . . . . . . . . . .127
152 Cradley Heath station . . . . . . . . . . . .127
153 The entrance to Old Hill . . . . . . . . .128
154 Sikh temple at Tividale . . . . . . . . . .128
155 West Bromwich Building
     Society advertisement . . . . . . . . . .129

# Acknowledgements

As a child, I heard Rowley Regis before I saw it, in the form of loud explosions from the quarry at 9, 12 and 3 o'clock. Later I taught at the grammar school, and began researching local history and collecting oral and written information. I taught WEA classes and seminars for teachers in the County Borough of Warley, in some cases learning as much as I taught. My pupils helped to copy gravestone inscriptions at Rowley church and St Luke's, and we were fortunate that the Rev. S.B. Coley allowed us to make transcripts of many damaged documents in the safe at Rowley church (later transferred to Sandwell archives).

Rowley Regis historians all owe a debt of gratitude to Ron Moss, who has pioneered and carefully steered industrial archaeology in the area, and published invaluable material on Old Hill and Cradley Heath, as well as Mushroom Green chainshop. Much information about the area was saved by Horace Wilson, at one time head of Beeches Road school, whose drawings of restorations are always of interest. The vicar of Rowley in the 1920s, F.C. Cheverton, collected and published in the parish magazine some material which would otherwise have been lost.

I have been aided by reminiscences of so many ex-pupils and students that I cannot mention them all, but I hope they will accept my grateful thanks.

I acknowledge with thanks the sources of the illustrations as follows. Every effort has been made to trace copyright where such exists; any inadvertent omissions will be remedied in a future edition.

Author's photographs or drawings: 1, 2, 5-14, 16, 19-21, 23-9, 33-9, 41-51, 53-61, 65, 70-7, 79-82, 84, 85, 90, 91, 102, 104, 106, 112, 113, 114, 117-20, 122, 124, 131, 133-5, 137, 138, 141, 148, 150-3; author's collection (advertisements): 139, 143, 144, 146, 154; author's collection: 3, 4, 52, 62-4, 66, 68, 83, 86, 95-9, 100, 105, 107, 127, 155; commercial postcards: 30, 69, 108; Courtesy of Philip Adams: 40, 109, 111, 125 142; Headteacher, Burnt Tree primary school: 17,

94, 100, 123; Roger Kite: 87, 88; Thomas Lench & Co.: 103; Metropolitan Borough of Dudley, ephemera: 92; Metropolitan Borough of Sandwell, ephemera: 22; Nash's *Worcestershire* (1799): 15; Newman College Resources (based on Dudley archives): 67; Rowley parish magazine, 1920ff: 18, 31, 42, 115, 116; Rowley Regis Grammar School Magazine and other publications: 126, 128-30, 132, 136; Rowley Regis UDC and Borough: 140, 145; John Southall: 32, 89, 110; Jean Ward (née Davies): 149; Keith Wellings: 121; David Willis, 78, 101.

# Earliest Times

tanding on the playing fields behind Hawes Lane, Rowley Regis, we look down on one of the most impressive scenes in the Black Country. Far below us in the valley we can see houses and workshops snaking away towards Stourbridge, a red and blue blur punctuated by green, with the Clent Hills to our left and the hazy distant Clees to our right. We can pick out landmarks such as the tower of Old Hill church and blocks of 20th-century flats at Riddings Mound and Cradley. As dusk settles, we see thousands of twinkling lights along the valley, seemingly miles away from the clear open air of the Rowley hills.

Yet much of what we see in the nearer distance is part of the historic parish of Rowley Regis, which became a borough in the mid-20th century and has now lost its independence as part of the Metropolitan

1   *The view looking south-west from near Tippity Green.*

Hadrian         Antoninus       Carausius       Constantine

2  *Four Roman coins similar to those found near the Hailstone.*

Borough of Sandwell. Outside the Midlands, the names of Cradley Heath, Old Hill, Black-heath and Tividale, the four towns which made up Rowley borough, do not mean much. Bordered on the north by Tipton, the east by Oldbury, the south by Halesowen and Cradley, and the west by Dudley and Quarry Bank, Rowley parish was a long finger of Staffordshire protruding into Worcestershire. Until the 19th century its population was sparse, but here were produced the iron to make anchors for the *Titanic*, nails to hold together Hampton Court, roadstone for tarmac to pave the Midlands and, at one time, the jews' harps for the whole of Great Britain and abroad.

The Rowley hills form part of the watershed which runs along the backbone of England. To the north, the limestone gives us the rock caverns of Dudley and the ridge of Sedgley Beacon but here in prehistoric times there was a volcanic eruption, which caused molten basalt to rise up through the strata and form the grey cap of Turner's Hill. Geologists became convinced of this when the Netherton Canal Tunnel was dug in the mid-19th century. This volcanic cap was greened over and has now become the pleasant grassy area for Dudley Golf Club. Under much of the parish lies the thick coal, 12 foot seams of 'black diamonds', unfortunately intersected with faults; there is also

fireclay and iron ore. These minerals began to be exploited in the Middle Ages, but it was the Industrial Revolution which speeded up the process and made these towns what they now are.

We know nothing of earlier populations, though we can speculate about the possibility of Iron-Age habitation on the heights of Turner's Hill, and wonder how old the track is which is still called Portway. There are some Celtic names in the area, such as Penncricket Lane leading towards Causeway Green, and we can reasonably conjecture that 'the Causeway' indicates an old embankment over low-lying ground. There have been no archaeological investigations of any of these sites. (The name of Turner's Hill seems to have developed through Torrell's from Turchill's.)

We are on firmer ground when we come to the Romans. Stebbing Shaw, the Staffordshire historian, writing in 1798, records the finding of a coin horde a few years previously:

> In 1794 was also found, in pulling down an old stone wall at Rowley Regis, an earthen globe containing about 1200 ... coins in silver which when all together formed a complete series of the Roman emperors ...

The Rowley curate, George Barrs, added later that the wall in question was 'a little to the

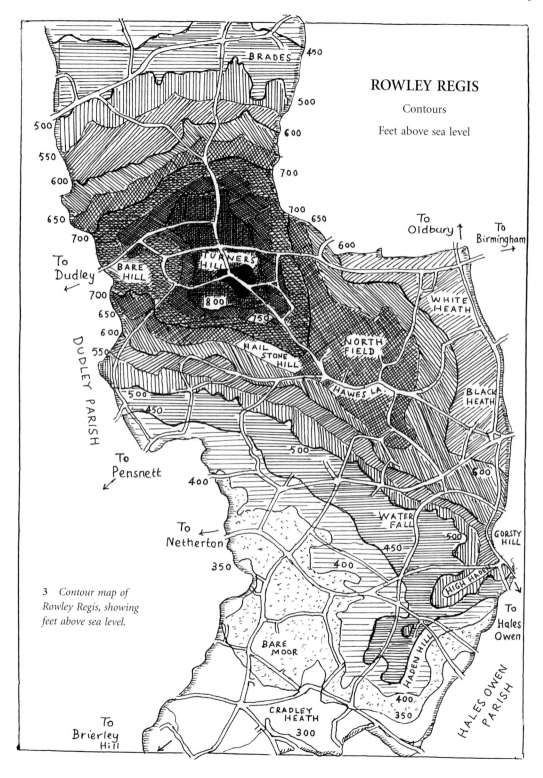

BRADES 450

500

500

550

600

600

650

700

To
Dudley

BARE
HILL

700

650

600

550

500

450

To
Pensnett

400

To
Netherton

350

**ROWLEY REGIS**

Contours

Feet above sea level

600

700

700 650

600

TURNER'S
HILL

800

750

HAIL
STONE
HILL

NORTH
FIELD

HAWES LA.

500

500

To
Oldbury ↑

To
Birmingham →

WHITE
HEATH

BLACK
HEATH

600

WATER
FALL

450

500

400

GORSTY
HILL

HIGH HADE

To
Hales
Owen

DUDLEY PARISH

BARE
MOOR

HADEN HILL

400

350

HALES OWEN PARISH

3  *Contour map of
Rowley Regis, showing
feet above sea level.*

CRADLEY
HEATH

300

To
Brierley
Hill

4   *The Hailstone, a natural rock formation.*

south-east of the Hailstone'. Just below the wall was a large stone 'a few inches thick', and the earthen vessel was under it, with a small slit at the top through which the Roman coins must have been posted. In all there had been seven hundred, but they were dispersed and their details apparently not recorded apart from the few belonging to the Vicar of Clent and Rowley. A further Roman horde was found ten years later at Cakemore, a mile beyond Rowley's eastern boundary. Could there have been Roman occupation in Rowley? It is just possible, and almost certain that traces of an ancient settlement of some kind might still be found. The search should focus on Higham's Hill, around Highmoor Road.

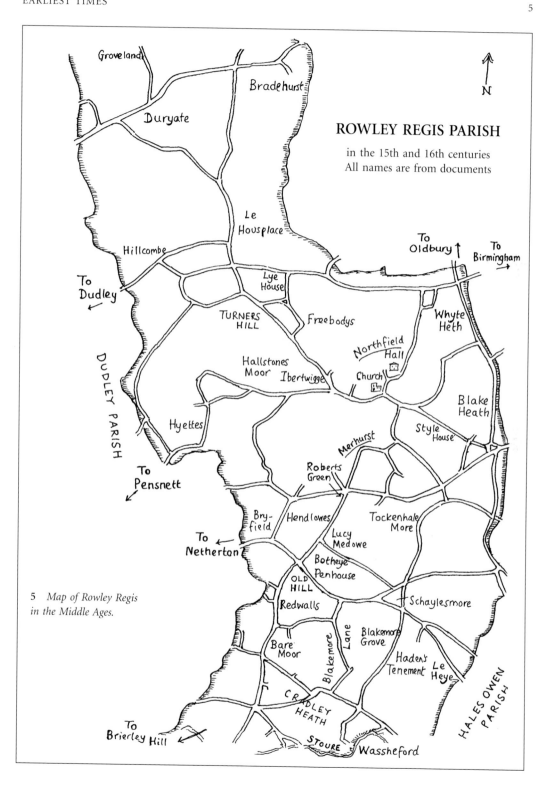

**ROWLEY REGIS PARISH**

in the 15th and 16th centuries
All names are from documents

5  Map of Rowley Regis
in the Middle Ages.

6   *Large pieces of Rowley rag, used as a barrier near Perry's Lake.*

At the time of the 1800 survey, fields bordering on what is now Moor Lane were called 'Camp Hawes'. Moor Lane drops steeply below the land to the north, as can be seen from the illustration on page 18. An early 18th-century deed describes this plot as 'Wallcroft' and gives in addition the name 'Camp House', which generally indicates a former settlement, and this may have been Roman. It is interesting that the site above the lane is quartered in the 1800 map, although the Latin second element in the place-name Rowley Regis has nothing to do with this. (There were Roman settlements at Metchley near Edgbaston, and Greensforge near Kingswinford, but the road linking them has not so far been discovered.)

Anglo-Saxons colonised Britain along the river valleys of the Trent and Severn. Here, on the watershed, it is difficult to know which tribe reached Turner's Hill first. The Angles from the direction of West Bromwich possibly looked down on the Saxons from Stourbridge. It is interesting that there is still a dialect difference between the south-west and north-east Black Country areas, and that Old Hill and Cradley Heath speak like Dudley and Stourbridge, while older residents of Rowley Village sound more like those from Oldbury. This underlines the parochial nature of the Black Country towns, breaking down nowadays but still observable. The old parishes here all extend from north to south, not east to west, and this is true of Tividale/Rowley/Cradley Heath, Oldbury/Halesowen and Smethwick/Harborne.

There is no mention of Rowley in Domesday, which is surprising, since all the other neighbouring towns are mentioned. Rowley has always been disputed between Worcester

7  *The boundary brook at Grovelands, straightened from its original winding course.*

and Stafford. It seems initially to have been part of Clent Hundred in Worcestershire, with Dudley, Halesowen and Oldbury, then the whole of the ancient parish of Clent, including Rowley, was placed in Staffordshire. Then Clent returned to Worcestershire, but Rowley stayed in Staffordshire, an anomaly as it was in Worcester Diocese, which may account for why there is no mention of Rowley in Domesday Book: it was still part of Clent. Clent, however, was very large; it contained nine 'hides' whereas Hagley had five and Northfield six.

It must have been at this time that the boundaries of Rowley were fixed. It is divided from Dudley by two brooks rising near Oakham (previously 'Holcum', the hollow combe), one, called at various points Meryhurst brook, Mousesweet brook and Newtown brook, flowing into the Stour and so to the Severn; the other, forming a boundary with Tipton parish, flowing into the Tame and thus the Trent. The meaning of 'Mousesweet' is very obscure. It has been thought that it indicated a place where the Saxon 'moot' assembled, but there is little evidence for this. 'Meryhurst' may indicate a boundary copse. On the south, Rowley is divided from Halesowen and Cradley by the Stour, and on the east by a boundary at the rear of Oldbury Road which is mysteriously straight as though it were a late modification. The whole of this parish area, with little change, survived as a single administrative unit from Norman times to the late 20th century.

Why, then, is the name of Rowley Regis half Latin? Kingswinford, Kings Norton and Kings Bromley are all sometimes 'Swinford Regis', 'Norton Regis' and 'Bromley Regis' in medieval and 16th-century documents,

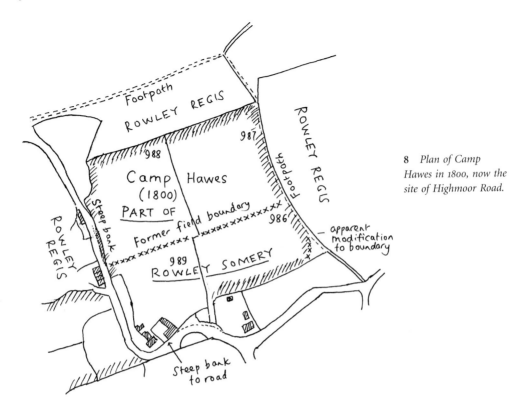

8  *Plan of Camp Hawes in 1800, now the site of Highmoor Road.*

but in those cases the Latin form died more quickly. In two documents of the mid-18th century Rowley is 'Rowley Kings'. Like the local places mentioned above, we can presume that Rowley was 'ancient demesne' of the king in the 11th century, i.e. before the Norman Conquest. This does not imply that the king went hunting in these places, but he had the right to do so and the presence of deer is witnessed by the old name of Tividale: 'Dereyate' (deer gate). At a later stage, part of Rowley became alienated from the Crown and formed another manor, Rowley Somery. Thus, although there was only one chapelry, there were two manors, which had to be distinguished one from the other: Rowley Somery and King's Rowley, or Rowley Regis. These two manors continued well into the 19th century. We shall be tracing their history and defining the geography as we follow them through the Middle Ages to the enclosure award. Today there is no definable Rowley Somery, but it has played its part over the years and should not be forgotten.

# II

# Reconstructing Medieval Rowley

Medieval villages were owned and administered by two authorities, sometimes conflicting. The medieval church, in the form of bishops and abbots, controlled spiritual life, while the king, represented by barons and lesser nobility, held power in the secular sphere. Their boundaries did not always coincide. Rowley was not ecclesiastically a parish (it is often called a 'chapelry') but was part of Clent. The two manors functioned separately, with different courts and customs. Few local records remain from these distant times, and we have to read back cautiously from later periods.

There is some help with the geography of the two manors in the 'court rolls' of each. These are supplemented by the schedule of the early 19th-century enclosure award. Early documents for Rowley Somery begin in the 16th century, while for the Regis manor there are court rolls as far back as the fourteenth. Between them they establish a confusing picture, of pieces of Rowley Somery scattered throughout the chapelry, and in the 18th century the members of the court gave up trying to walk the boundaries, as should have been done. They said that their manor 'lies so promiscuously within the Manor … of Rowley Regis … that it is too hard for

9  *Mincing Lane: the former farmhouse. The name may mean 'the nuns' lane'.*

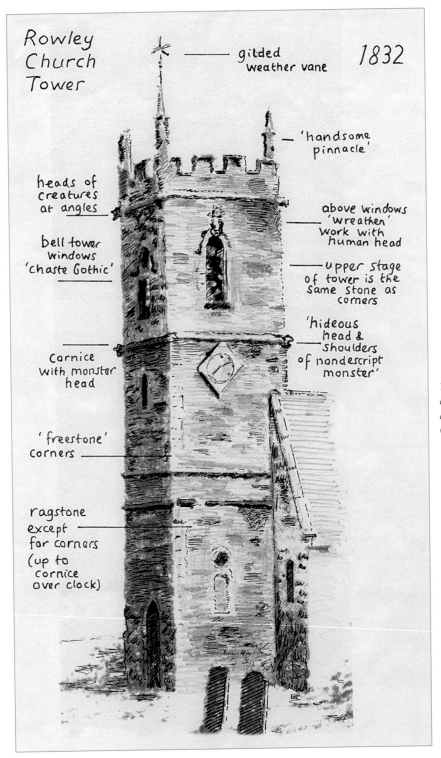

Rowley Church Tower

1832

gilded weather vane

'handsome pinnacle'

heads of creatures at angles

bell tower windows 'chaste Gothic'

above windows 'wreathen' work with human head

upper stage of tower is the same stone as corners

'hideous head & shoulders of nondescript monster'

Cornice with monster head

'freestone' corners

ragstone except for corners (up to cornice over clock)

10 *The original church tower as described by George Barrs.*

us to meet and bound the same as it ought to be done'. Broadly speaking, we can say that the majority of Rowley Somery lay at Windmill End, Knowle, Rowley, along both sides of Powke Lane and at Waterfall. There were small enclaves at Bearmore and Brades, and one or two other detached pieces. Rowley Regis included most of Cradley Heath, Whiteheath, Haden Hill, much of Old Hill and Tividale.

There is confusion about who owned each manor. Documents belonging to the Dudley family show that it was Regis which they owned in the 14th century, though Somery was one of their family names. Henry II granted Rowley Regis to the de Rushales in 1154, and this was ratified by King John in 1200. The de Rushales are probably the ancestors of the later Russell family who owned Portway Hall. From 1227 to 1255 there are law suits in which the Somery family sue the

Rushales for two carucates of land. In 1269 a widowed member of the Rushale family was attacked in her house with weapons by a group of marauders. In the latter part of the 13th century the manor passed through a series of hands, though a jury at Seisdon in 1293 declared that the manor was 'of ancient demain' and belonged to the Somerys. By 1316 John de Somery was certainly the owner of Regis. The Abbot of Halesowen apparently rented it in 1330, paying directly to the King in 1337. The oldest record of the Somery manor, on the other hand, seems to be 1532.

It is also difficult to say when St Giles' church was built. The traditional date is 1199, and the reign of King John seems likely, but a precise date may never be found. It is quite possible that an earlier church stood on the site, though a place name ending in -ton rather than -ley would have been a clearer indication of early settlement. The original

11   *The stump of Haden Cross, now in Haden Hill Park.*

**12**   *Notice describing Warrens Hall Park; the Dudley Road at the north is a 19th-century innovation.*

**13**   *The site of Warren's Hall in 1960. The line of the moat can be seen just in front of the group of trees, and the farm pond is marked by a depression behind the tall tree.*

14  *Nineteenth-century cottage at Warren's Hall, 1960.*

Rowley Hall could have been built at about this time. An inquisition of 1327 found that there was a 'messuage' (significant house) here, but it was in ruins. However, there is a site which has as good a claim to antiquity, namely Warren's Hall. This was probably not the manor house for the Regis manor, but it could have been an independent fortified house. A field near the hall was called Moat Leasow, and there were certainly signs of a depression there in living memory. The hall became a farmhouse and was demolished in the 19th century; it is therefore impossible to guess its age. Cradley Mill is mentioned as early as 1179 and a number of times in the 13th century; at the death of Roger de Somery in 1272 an inquisition mentions the mill 'de Ruleye'.

The settlement at Haden Hill also dates from this time. The origin of this name

may be Anglo-Saxon *Hege* plus *denu*, the valley in the enclosure. Hayseech, next to it, means the small stream in the enclosure. The Haden family take their name from this place, as also may the Addenbrook (originally 'Adenebrok') family (from 'Haden brook'). Earliest evidence is from about 1270, when land is granted to the Hadens by Philip de Rushale, lord of the Regis manor. The family were already powerful, extending their estates to where much later there would be a fortune to be made from coal.

In 1291 a short manorial survey gives us the names of a number of Rowley residents. They include Richard and Roger de Derybate, Thomas de Wynesthurst, Philip ate Toun, John le Fevre, Philip de Brodehurst, John Martyn, Henry de Muryhurst and Stephen ate Hade. Of the six place-names from which these men take their surnames, Derybate is now Tividale

**15**  *Halesowen Abbey, from Nash's* Worcestershire. *The abbey owned part of Rowley Regis.*

**16**  *Rowley church about 1803, based on a drawing by David Parkes.*

Hall, Wynesthurst Farm (later Wince Farm) nearly opposite it, Brodehurst, The Brades, and Hade is Haden Hill. 'Toun' is of course Rowley Town, or Rowley Village, and shows that there was already a small settlement on the hillside there. At this time the manor house, Rowley Hall, was worth 2s.

A tax document of 1327 (the 'subsidy') gives the names of the main inhabitants of Rowley. Those mentioned above have been joined by 'atte Grave', 'de Tukkenhale', and 'de Scaresmore', their residences being respectively at Grovelands, Totnal (near Powke Lane) and possibly near Old Hill, though the last one is very uncertain. There are also Philip atte Wode, John Orm, Richard son of Thomas and others. Some of the same names occur in 14th-century court rolls, with other men called Whyte and Wyllenhalle. A Rowley jury of 1450 consisted of the following people (partly modernised spelling): Thomas Staresmore, John Derby, William Adynbroke, Thomas Turhull, William Grove, Roger Derby, William Cook, William Alnechurch, William Haden, William Adynrok jnr, John Orme.

Estate boundaries were probably marked by stone crosses like the one at Haden Cross, the base of which is still to be seen at Haden Hill. Thus we have the preserving name of Old Hill Cross, the almost obsolete example at Lye Cross (*not* the one at Lye, but near the *Wheatsheaf* on Turner's Hill), and the completely forgotten one at Derickton Cross (Tividale). Roads were generally poor, but some effort must have been made to keep them up since they led to markets as well as political and religious assembly points. In 1466 the Abbot of Hales is allowed land in 'le Hille' and Whiteheath on condition that the convent makes and maintains a gate at le Hille and two gates at 'Whyteheth', across the highway leading to Birmingham, Walsall,

17   *Tividale Hall, from a souvenir programme at the opening of the park.*

Dudley, Oldbury and other places, and allows these highways for walking, riding, and any other kind of business without hindrance at all times. The place name 'Whiteheath Gate' therefore has a very long pedigree. There was no direct route across Warren's Hall from Rowley to Dudley; instead, at the Hailstone the road turned south and led to Pensnett.

Among places named in the 15th-century court rolls are 'Bradest' (Brades), 'Duryate-land' (probably the road through Tividale), 'Ladylye' near Lye Cross, 'Squyarmore', part of later Squire's Tenement, near Windmill End, 'Blakemore Lane', 'Wassheford' (the Stour near Corngreaves), and the Hall Meadow and 'Hallemore', presumably behind Rowley Village. A croft just south of Wright's Lane on Old Hill High Street (Highgate Street) is 'Botheye', and to the north of this, on the other side of Wright's Lane, is 'Lucymedowe'. Blackheath ('Blakeheth') is mentioned in 1483, and there is a group of fields called Mitteleys and Turhuleshull towards the top of what is now City Road. ('Turhuleshull' is presumably the name which developed into 'Turner's Hill'.)

We should imagine a scene of scattered holdings and cottages with wooden frames, perhaps infilled with stone. Probably only at Rowley Village was there a group of buildings surrounding the hall and church. Behind the church was one of the open fields where the peasants farmed in strips. Another field was probably below the hall, on the slope leading towards Bell End. A brook, now lost, ran down this slope and possibly filled the pool which used to be in Britannia Park and may have been a fish pond: medieval England needed fish to eat on Fridays, and there were no trout streams on the Rowley hills. The name 'Mincing Lane' means 'the nuns' lane', and we might look for a small convent somewhere in this area but, so far, no such place has been found.

# III

# Tudors and Stuarts

The status of 'ancient demain' seems to have persuaded King Henry VIII to grant a charter to the chapelry in 1524, freeing the inhabitants from jury service outside Rowley and from some taxes. A translation made in 1741 was called upon as evidence when attempts to reinstate these freedoms were made in the 20th century. All such considerations were swamped in the upheaval which took place after Henry began to revolutionise England's relations with Rome. To prepare for possible war against Spain, he caused a survey to be undertaken in 1539 in which inhabitants would declare what arms they had in preparation for the fight. Fifteen men of Rowley claimed to have weapons stored at home. They were William Orme, Henry a Whille, John Grove, John Darby, Thomas Russell, Thomas Cartwright, Richard Haden, Thomas Hawtrun, George Allchurch, Thomas Parkes, Henry Cattell, George Marten, John Mansell, John Hoccheks(Hodgetts?) and John Addenbroke. Some had swords, others daggers, bills and a set of bows and arrows. Twenty-six years later, when Thomas Willetts made his will, he was able to pass on to his brother 'my sword and dagger'.

Halesowen Abbey was dissolved in 1538 and the contents of the building dispersed in the following year. Abbey lands passed to

18  *Sir John Turton, descendant of the Turtons of Rowley Regis and West Bromwich, engraved in 1707.*

Lord Dudley, Duke of Northumberland, a major player on the national stage. There was turmoil in the land, with secular authorities confiscating church property and the nobility trying to exploit the chaotic circumstances. In 1552 King Edward VI's assessors paid a visit to Rowley church and found that it possessed 'one challes of silver with a patent; one old vestment of dunne silke; one cope of blewe velvet; two copes of grene silke; one crosse

17

of brasse in gilt; four bells'. The church had recently been repaired with the proceeds of the sale of two brass candlesticks for 8d.

The gentry and nobility were litigious; one suit brought by Dame Mary Leveson against William Orme, concerned his lease of 'Bradeshurste' (The Brades), which he produced in court to show it dated from 1547. Lord Dudley's stewards decided in 1556 to survey the manor of Rowley Regis and produce a detailed rent roll. Some of the most significant holdings were William Colborne's White Heath (part of the abbey lands), William Ireland's 'Freebody's' (later Freebury farm), William Hill's 'Torrells' (land on the northern slope above Tividale), and land held by Richard Haden, including Luce Meadow near what is now Wright's Lane. Cradley Heath was an open stretch, uncultivated, and villagers from Cradley, in the next manor, had the right to feed cattle on

it. Sir Richard Leveson's right to the Brades is confirmed in this survey. Among other places whose names have survived to this day are Bare Moor, 'Bryfield', which became Bluebell farm, and Grovelands.

By this time the area had a strong trade in hand-made nails. It is said that Dudley nails were supplied to Hampton Court Palace, and there is evidence of distant trade in the Rowley will of Thomas Willetts, who was owed money when he died in 1565 by two gentlemen of Reading, two of Oxford, one of 'Abentun' (Abingdon) and one of Maidstone. In turn he owed local men about £6 10s. This suggests that he was buying nails from these middlemen and transporting them, perhaps by packhorses, to the south of England. Nailers make frequent appearances in wills and the county court records: for example, John Bridgewater, nailer, is alleged to have stolen three pairs of sheets, four silver spoons, a

**19**   *The steep slope of Moor Lane. On the right is the bank below Camp Hawes.*

covering and a platter from Isabel and William Cartwright in 1591. A statute of 1563 forbade nailing unless there had been seven years' apprenticeship, but in time we find most inhabitants of Rowley supplementing their income from minor agriculture with small profits from nailing. Another trade seems to have been in Rowley stone: when Richard Martin died in 1591 he left '19 [loads?] blowe [blue] stone and 2 half loads'.

The Gunpowder Plot had an impact in Rowley. Primary evidence is hard to gather, but it seems that two plotters escaping from Holbeach House in November 1605 were sheltered here by villagers called Smart and Christopher White. The conspirators, Robert Winter and Stephen Littleton, are said to have been hidden in Rowley until New Year's Day and it has been suggested it was at Rowley Hall that the plotters hid. A Richard Smart witnessed a will in 1595, but no one called Smart appears in Rowley registers before 1655. A Christopher White, who may have been the plotter, was buried in 1611, and there are other members of the White family whose wills are available during the last part of the 16th century. It is not clear where they lived, but 'White's Tenement' is later said to be at the Yew Tree; they do not appear to have had the status to inhabit Rowley Hall.

A major landholder at the time, with holdings in both the Regis and Somery manors, was William Orme. His will gives typical examples of the network of family relations which sustained the higher as well as the lower members of society. He has links with the less prestigious members of the Dudley family, leaving his 'kinswoman' Margaret Dudley the Brickhouse (now the site of Brickhouse Estate) and a farm tenanted by John Bridgwater called Martin's farm. He leaves land to another relative, William Orme of West Bromwich, including his own dwelling

20   *Stone outbuildings at Haden Hill.*

21   *The old font at Rowley church, broken in a fire.*

22   *The Oak House, West Bromwich, home of the Turton family.*

somewhere in the Ross area. He has land in Wombourne and Penn, which he leaves to another relative, Richard Jevon; both Upper and Lower Penn are associated with Rowley Somery and later have the same steward. He leaves Roger Allchurch, descendant of one of the armed men of 1539, five closes and a pasture, and another relative, William Steward, 'the ffoulters field' which had been owned by Philip Orme in the 1556 rent roll. John Turton (related to the West Bromwich Turtons) inherits 'Swaynes Croft', near Powke Lane. A house, possibly near Brades, is given to William Hunt. The will itemises the precise yield per annum of each holding. It is financially detailed, and suggests a Protestant entrepreneur. William wished to be buried inside the church under a marble slab.

The will and inventory of Roger Parkes, giving his occupation as 'nailer', shows how small-scale agriculture was mixed with nailing at this time. Roger (who owned a 10s. Bible) left benches and 'stocks' with his smithy tools, including two pairs of bellows, to his sons Roger and William. To his married daughter he left a sheep and to another son a ewe. He had an acre of barley on the ground, with some barley and rye already harvested on 13 June 1613 when his inventory was taken. A likely location for him is Waterfall Lane, but this is conjecture. He left debts of 16s., with 22s. owing to him, and had 3s. 4d. in his purse. Other Rowley residents had cows they called by name: John Turhill, who died in 1566, had one called 'Ffylpayle', and a calf called 'Daybell'.

There were by now a number of mills in Rowley. The River Stour, though relatively small, provided enough power to drive mills at Cradley, higher up at Hedger's Mill, and possibly at Hayseech. In 1621 Humphrey Wall of Cradley let to a man from 'Yarnton' (probably Erdington), Warwickshire 'One Mill House … and all barns, buildings, gardens, orchards, lands and heriditaments … and a close, pasture or parcel of ground … known as Smithy Crofte … all in the occupation of John Hedges or his assigns'. When his descendant Edward Hedger died in 1671, the mill house had two rooms and a buttery, with the mill itself storing such things as crowbars and some corn and hay. His possession of 'straw for thetching' also reveals the roofing method, which was no doubt common. A little further downstream was Cradley Forge, where Dud Dudley discovered a method of smelting iron with coal instead of charcoal and patented it in 1620.

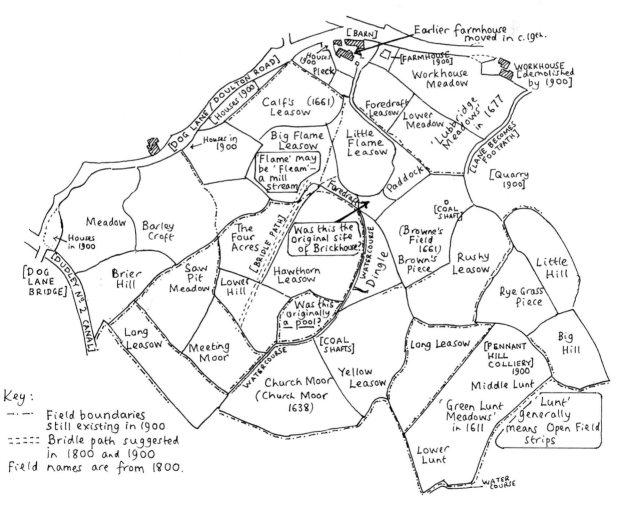

23   Plan of the estate at Brickhouse, showing changes from 1800 to 1900. This helps determine the possible location of the original house.

**24** *Portway Hall in the early 1960s.*

Political and religious conflict characterised the mid-17th century. It seems that most local inhabitants, with their trading background, supported Parliament. The parish registers suffer no serious break, and when a change in procedure demands that wedding banns are declared in a market town, not church, Walsall is chosen as the town. Details of weddings, which took place at Hamstead, are entered in the register, but it seems that infant baptism continued, so that dates of birth (as recommended) were not substituted for dates of christening. Only one landowner is reported as a suspected Royalist in 1648: William Brimfield of Derrett Hall (variously spelt, i.e. Tividale Hall). From 1654 to 1662 William Turton was the minister.

The Turton family is prominent in the history of West Bromwich, Rowley and other local parishes. An early residence is at Grovelands, apparently the home of a John Turton of Rowley who married Joan Rogers in 1540.

Branches continued at West Bromwich, but descendants also lived at Alrewas, and it is from them that John Turton the judge was descended. William, the minister, was baptised at Oxford and attended Brasenose College. His tenure at Rowley became insecure after the Restoration, and he was ejected under the Act of Uniformity, later becoming minister at the Old Meeting in Birmingham.

A number of statistical and other enquiries took place in the latter half of the 17th century. In 1661 came the demand that churches should give a detailed account of the state of their buildings and people. The churchwardens responded that the church fabric was 'in good and decent order' and that none of the goods had been 'sold or embezzled'. The churchyard was fenced 'with a stone wall' – evidence that Rowley ragstone was in use for walling locally. The minister's house was 'in good repair', and the curate was regular and used the Book of Common

Prayer. The inhabitants were good attenders and there were no nonconformists. Only Edward Harrison refused to come to church, and two members of the Parkes family had been excommunicated. There were no hospitals or schools, but Ambrose Crowley practised 'Chyrurgery'. (This is confirmed at his death in 1680, when he gives his trade as 'nailer', but possesses 'chyrurgery' tools in his inventory. One hopes he kept his fire tongs separate from his surgeon's implements!) This particular churchwardens' return gives the impression of being a whitewash.

In the 1660s a new form of levy was introduced: Hearth Tax. Among the important inhabitants on the assessment list were John Bissell of 'Hyams Hill', Richard Carpenter of 'Salters Tenement' (Mincing Lane), John and William Cartwright of the Knowle, widow Coley of Waterfall, Henry Haden of Haden Hill (also known as 'Hill Purlieu'), Edward Hedger (the miller of Hedger's Mill), Thomas 'Mininges' (Monins)

of Tividale Hall, George Norbury of Cradley Heath, Jane and John Parkes of Hyams Hill, Richard and Roger Parkes of Waterfall, Jonathan Rushton of Windmill End, the Russells of Portway Hall, John Turton of the Brades, three men called Thomas Willetts, at Portway, Oakham, and at 'the Hall', and William Woodhouse of Brickhouse. In 1674 William Russell rebuilt Portway Hall, if the monogram over the door of the now demolished house (W.A.R. 1674) means William and Alice Russell, 1674.

The Rowley Somery manor court met in 1670 to survey the Somery lands. The chief landholders were Richard Amphlett, proprietor of Warren's Hall, Richard Aynsworth at the Yew Tree (White's Tenement), John Dabbs (Dobbs' Bank) and Jonathan Rushton near Windmill End. This was the last time an accurate survey of Rowley Somery was made for a considerable while, the court administration apparently falling into a state of neglect towards the end of the century.

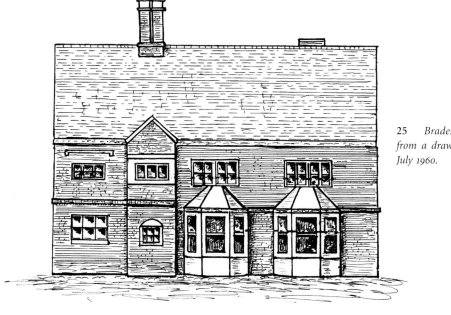

25   *Brades Hall farm, from a drawing made in July 1960.*

26    *A stone wall at Rowley Hall, possibly the foundation of the original hall.*

27    *Entrance to Portway Hall, with the date stone 1674 and monogram of William and Alice Russell.*

Six years later the Bishop of Worcester sent out a questionnaire to try to gather church statistics. The main question concerned the total number of inhabitants, but numbers of papists and dissenters were also required for what was called the Compton Return. The same number, 420, appears in both the churchwardens' own notes and the final return, but it cannot possibly be right. Other methods of calculating, using the registers of baptisms and deaths, clearly show that there must have been nearer 1500. Just possibly the return misses off the first '1', but it has to be said that other returns from neighbouring parishes are sometimes faulty. The churchwardens, Henry Warren and Joseph Tonks, add that 384 'absent themselves but not obstinately', but this sentence does not occur in the final Compton Return and, even if they are added, the total is too low. In such a scattered parish, with hilly paths and disjointed communities, it may be that church attendance from those outside the village was very poor. The churchwardens certainly seem to be hiding something, and this may have been the indifference of some of the richer residents; Henry Haden had been reported in 1674 for not having his children baptised and George Colborne was 'permitting private meetings in his house' (i.e. dissenting religious meetings).

By 1684 it is clear that the church needed substantial repair. In June the churchwardens report that the chancel needs work, and later that year we find that the bells are being renewed and re-hung. In October, 'the chancel will be got in good order as soon as materials are found'. Four bells were either recast or purchased new that year. Inscriptions on them stated 'Henry Bayliss made me', 'Mathew Bagley of Chalcombe made me', and the tenor was given by William Staremore. This, at any rate, is the name recorded years

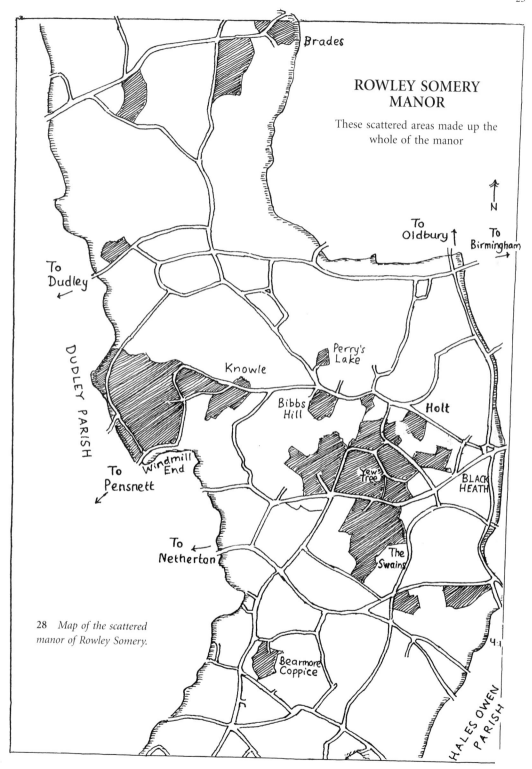

**ROWLEY SOMERY MANOR**

These scattered areas made up the whole of the manor

Brades

To Oldbury

To Birmingham

N

To Dudley

DUDLEY PARISH

To Pensnett

Perry's Lake

Knowle

Bibbs Hill

Holt

Windmill End

Yew Tree

BLACK HEATH

To Netherton

The Swains

28 Map of the scattered manor of Rowley Somery.

Bearmore Coppice

HALES OWEN PARISH

after by the curate George Barrs, though a drawing gives the name as 'Stavenor'. There were no Stavenors in Rowley, but there had been an influential family called Staresmore, the head of which now lived at Monks Kirby in Leicestershire.

In the final decade of the century concern seems to have arisen over the educational and religious state of the parish. It should be remembered that Rowley was still deemed part of Clent for church purposes, and the Vicar of Clent, Thomas Walker, had occupied the post since at least 1669. The churchwardens reported in 1693 that there was no curate. There was no free school in Rowley, and a certain Birmingham schoolmaster, Mr Foster, would come over to perform 'the services of the lane'. Elizabeth Brimfield of Derretts Hall (Tividale), 'Dame' Elizabeth Monins since her second marriage to Thomas Monins, a

Kentish nobleman, set up a group of trustees in 1703 to remedy the lack of a school. She did not live long enough to see the results of her important action, making her will two years later and being buried on 6 November 1705. By this time Rowley had a curate, the Rev. Thomas Garratt.

If the provisions of her will were enacted, 6 November 1705 must have been a spectacular day in Rowley. The funeral procession started in Tividale from a house hung throughout with mourning black. The coffin was covered with black velvet and trimmed with white sarsnett in a hearse pulled by six horses. The hearse was attended by a funeral coach, also pulled by six horses, with the school trustees riding inside. The journey up the lane across what is now Tividale Park and along the steep Upper City Road to the cross roads, then down the now vanished lane across Turner's

29   *Haden Hill restoration notice.*

**30** *'Tudor House', Haden Hill; there has always been uncertainty about the name of Haden Hall, or Haden Hill House.*

Hill, must have taken hours, and the villagers would surely have turned out in force when the hearse and mourning coach reached Rowley Village. At the old church the pulpit was hung with black, with Lady Monins' 'escutcheon' in the centre. She wished a monument to be set up by her executors to record her gifts to the people of Rowley, the school endowment and a further £10 to the poor. Charity boards were eventually fixed to the church wall, but they do not survive.

How far these wishes of Lady Monins were carried out is not clear. We must remember that her august relatives lived in London and Kent (she lists in her will the houses she owned in the London area). She appointed Thomas Short, her niece's husband, as executor, and within a short time he had sold Derrett's Hall to the Turton family. Her legacy does not seem to have been enough to build a school and, as we shall see, the money fell into private hands.

IV

# The Eighteenth Century

Rowley people in the early 18th century seem to have been almost as divided as they were in the days of Cromwell and King Charles II. The Old Pretender's foray into northern England stayed far away from the Midlands, but high and low church affiliation remained an issue. In 1714 it was reported that one of the churchwardens, John Haden, had gone away on a long journey. We may wonder if this was to help against the rebellion?

Matters came to a head in 1717, when claim and counter-claim were made to the Bishop of Worcester in presentments at the visitation held at Bromsgrove. On the one hand, John Turton (we recall this family's Puritan tradition) and Henry Haden said that the curate, Thomas Saunders, had broken 'our antient custome' by choosing a churchwarden from the Nether side of the parish, when he should have chosen him from the Upper side, and there was a string of other charges

31 *Portway Farm in the 1960s. It is little changed now.*

**32** *Hailstone Farm about 1960. In the centre is the part-stone barn, with the 19th-century cottages beyond. On the right is the farmhouse.*

against him: he had begun a quarrel at the communion table, using very bad language; he had been carrying out clandestine marriages in the church, taking exorbitant fees; he had gone to law against '60 or 70' of the poor people in the parish and virtually ruined them; he had been reluctant to pray for King George; and possibly worst of all, he had 'in the late Rebelliouse and Tumultuouse tymes' refused to condemn the rebellion, and had caused people to desert the church, doubtless in favour of nonconformist gatherings.

Thomas Saunders countered that Henry Haden, although a churchwarden, had refused the sacrament and had spent the service time reading pamphlets and abusing him at the communion table. John Turton had committed perjury. Saunders did not enjoy his life among the spirited Rowley men, and his parting shot was that John Gaunt had been feeding his cows in the church porch. (An earlier visitation noted that this had been rebuilt from the ground in brick in 1708.) We do not know how the dispute was settled,

but on the whole it looks like evidence of a low church or Puritan stance on the part of influential residents.

The holding of courts at Rowley Somery had fallen into abeyance and it was decided 1717 to try to sort out the problem, a survey being made to work out what had happened to the land. Since the last court about twenty landholders had died, so failing to pay the normal fees to the lord of the manor. There was even a problem about where to hold the court, as there seemed to be no common land on which it could be legally assembled. The jurors finally concluded that the traditional space was at Barehill near Oakham. They managed to find about fifteen freeholders and three leaseholders. Not until 1755, when George Holyoak was appointed steward of Upper and Lower Penn as well as Rowley Somery, did better organisation arrive in the Somery manor.

The impression gained is of a population going its own way, not easily governed, clashing with high church clergymen and forgetful

**33**    *The site of Cradley Forge, once operated by Dud Dudley.*

**34**    *The old homestead at Oakham (formerly 'Holcombe').*

of legal detail. A great deal can be learned about them from wills and from information about their dwellings given in the registers. Rowley continued to be a parish of scattered hamlets, with only Rowley Village containing significant numbers of people. Many gave their occupation as 'nailer', and almost all inventories show a nailshop. The nailer's life was a hard one, but the income should be seen as a supplement to the cows and pigs in the 'backside'. Christopher Chambers of the Brickhouse owned 11 cows and two calves, six horses and two store pigs, but he still had a nail shop with its stocks and steadies.

There were other trades too. Thomas Bate of Tippity Green was a ropier. In the room over his main living quarters he had hemp and small cords, and he had a tar shop, with furnace, tar and working tools. Benjamin Plant lived in Hart's Tenement at Cradley

Heath, gave his trade as brickmaker, and had a handsaw and a framing saw among his tools. His son John also gave brick-making as his trade, but in the room over his warehouse he held a stock of flaxen cloth (37 ells) and he had a nailshop with a bellows and carpentry tools. He may have been a builder, with the capacity to make his own bricks as well as the wooden sections of a house, which suggests that there were houses to be built in the area, and in turn implies increasing prosperity.

At the northernmost end of the parish a family called Nicklin lived at Grovelands on the Tipton border. A low-lying track led from their farmhouse to Tividale, where there was a number of cottages strung along the Oldbury

35 *Cottage at Oakham, no. 361 on the 1800 plan, showing timber frame construction. It was photographed in 1960.*

36 *Old houses at Carnegie Road, Blackheath.*

MY ROARING SOVND DOTH
WARNING GIVE THAT MEN
CANNOT ALWAYES LIVE

1684

WILLIAM STARESMOR GAVE MEE TO THE TOWNE OF ROWLEY

37    *One of the church bells from 1684.*

to Dudley Road. The Turtons lived at the Brades, and it seems likely that the *Blue Ball* was already acting as an inn. From here, the narrow road up the north slope of Turner's Hill led to Portway. Here was Lyehouse Farm and, further along the road, Portway Hall. It was increasingly hard to find vestiges of the medieval open fields near Rowley Village; stray animals were caught and kept in the village pound near the end of Hall Lane.

From the inventories we can tell much about the interior of some of the cottages and farmhouses of the time. Most had a main room called the 'hall', with a fire grate and implements to stoke the fire. There were rush-seated chairs and long forms for the children. When the cloth was laid and pewter cups, plates and porringers set out, the scene was a very homely one. Several inventories mention bibles, which would be read aloud, but to judge by the number of testators who sign with an X, literacy was not always to be expected. Next to the hall was a parlour, where less important members of the family might sleep on a flock bed. The best beds were railed, and upstairs would often be a jumble of old boxes, chests, coffers, shelves and bushels of corn and oats, and wool awaiting carding; spinning wheels are a frequent feature. At Rowley Hall the Grove family owned silver plate and Mr John Grove would put on his riding habit and best pair of boots, and then go hunting across the hills with his pack of hounds.

38    *Former lane at Turner's Hill, photographed in 1962. Note the paving of Rowley rag.*

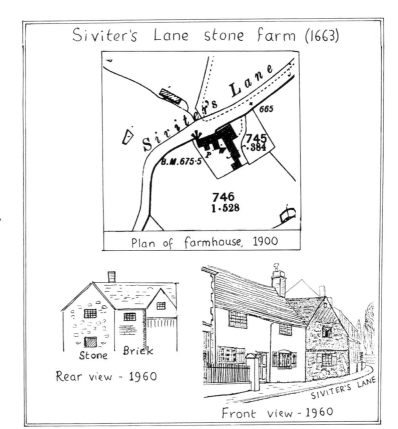

**39**  *The stone house in Siviter's Lane, dated 1663, now demolished.*

**40**  *Houses at Rowley Village, showing the stone arch and cottage property (demolished).*

**41**   *The poet James Woodhouse, from Rowley parish magazine.*

From the village one could descend Moor Lane towards Old Hill and Cradley Heath. There were farms at Totnal, Penhouse, Bryfield and beyond Old Hill Cross at Bearmore. The Gaunt family lived at Fox Oak Green House from mid-century on, beyond which came the expanse of Cradley Heath itself and the mill settlements along the Stour at Cradley Forge and Hedger's Mill. Nearer Halesowen stood the Hadens' stately home, already in the form we see today.

Communication between these scattered farms was rough but it was especially important that nails could be transported in bulk between Rowley, Old Hill and the two market towns of Dudley and Bromsgrove. In 1727 the roads were so muddy and full of rubbish that it was almost impossible to travel to town, and in winter it was out of the question. Henry Haden and both older and younger John Groves joined Thomas Haden and the lordly clergyman Thomas Saunders as trustees of the new turnpike, and the final seal on the Act of Parliament was set at Halesowen in early May 1727.

```
Order Nº 27  Cont.ᵈ 73
Bagging of Nailes & Baggen Cont
Dogg Nailes          D 20
Flat head Nailes     H
Flat pointed from 9tb to 36th  S
Flat pointed from 2 upwards    VX
Flat pointed strong  IP
Ditto short          IP
Tenter hooks         TH·IX
Lyne hooks           Lt·ev
Horse nailes long    H. 18
Lead Nailes          L7
Pound Nailes short   P15
Pound Nailes long    P. 14
Port nailes          P 80
```

**42**   *Types of nail in a list from the 17th century.*

One Rowley celebrity born in the 18th century was James Woodhouse, known as 'the Cobbler Poet'. It is generally thought that his birthplace was at Portway, and certainly some of the family did live there, having apparently inherited a small farm from James' grandmother, Mary Willetts. His grandfather John also occupied Sidaway's Close in Old Hill. James Woodhouse was baptised at Rowley church on 18 April 1735, and it is said that that he attended a local school which may have been the one set up by Lady Monins. He grew to be a very hefty man and soon set out to seek patronage, which he discovered in the shape of William Shenstone, the Halesowen poet. Tradition says that after working as a shoemaker he kept a school locally. His first published poem appears to have been an elegy dedicated to Shenstone, written in 1759. He travelled frequently to London, possibly as a deliverer of goods and packages, though he does not seem to have settled there, spending his time instead at Shenstone's estate, The Leasowes, where he is said to have helped to lay out the grounds.

Woodhouse's book, *Poems on Sundry Occasions*, was published in 1764. At this time he met Samuel Johnson, who remained rather unimpressed, commenting, 'He may make a good shoemaker, but he can never make a good poet.' Woodhouse took up a post as land bailiff to Edward Montague in Yorkshire, but was dismissed because of his democratic views. He moved back to the Midlands, and was land steward to Lord Lyttelton at Hagley. This post did not last long and he went back to London, writing further poems which he published in 1803 and 1804. He died in 1820 and was buried in London.

**43** *Houses at Dobbs Bank, which take the names of a 17th-century occupant.*

**44** *The former Style (or 'Stile') House Farm, now the* Britannia Inn. *Earlier photographs show chimneys at both ends.*

45   *Shops and houses to the north of Siviter's Lane, including 18th-century cottages, showing the variety of buildings in Rowley Village during the 1960s.*

46   *Blue Bell Farm in Old Hill; the name gradually changed from 'Bryfield'.*

Rowley church continued to be a place where power was exercised. To have a pew there constituted respectability, which is why arguments broke out over proprietorship. One such was between the Rayboulds, who owned Bryfield (Blue Bell Farm) in Old Hill, and Samuel Edwards. In late 1765 this took the form of scuffles in the gallery. Before the service started William Raybould went up to Samuel Edwards and 'irreverently, furiously and passionately' laid hands on his collar and tried to remove him forcibly from the seat which Raybould considered he had a right to. On Sunday 20 October Edwards retaliated, bringing some henchmen and 'shoving and pushing' Raybould out of his seat. This time it was Edwards who grabbed his enemy's collar and pulled him towards the exit. During the hearing at the Consistory Court, Edwards claimed to have been

**47**   The Robert Peel, *once a farmhouse belonging to the Mackmillan family.*

**48**   *Stone cottage in Hawes Lane, 1960. Many buildings in Rowley were made wholly or partly of stone.*

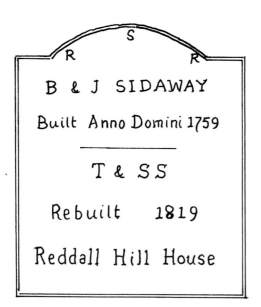

**49** *Plaque at 'Reddall Hill House', reconstructed from notes made in the 1960s. Reddal was often spelt 'Reddall' in olden days.*

a resident in Rowley for seven years and to have a prior right to the seat. We do not know the outcome of the quarrel, but ten years later another member of the Raybould family bought a seat in the middle aisle of the church, perhaps compensating for the lost gallery pew.

Such arguments were not confined to the inside of the church. On 5 July 1774 a row broke out in the churchyard. This may also echo factionalism among the population, for here Richard Gaunt was pitted against Daniel Bridgwater. Gaunt lived in a house near the church, at the end of Hawes Lane. Later he ran a school there, and an enquiry found that he was being paid Lady Elizabeth Monins' charity money. He set himself up as sexton (though not apparently to dig graves himself), whereas Bridgwater claimed to have been elected sexton by the parishioners, something alleged by Gaunt to be illegal. Gaunt also became parish clerk.

The occasion of the row was the burial of a stillborn child. Early on the July morning Richard Gaunt went to a gravedigger called Josiah Smith and told him to dig a grave. This was done, but when Daniel Bridgwater arrived he filled it in again. That afternoon both Gaunt and Bridgwater arrived in the churchyard with spades. Bridgwater asked, 'Is there a grave to be dug?' and the reply was, 'I have dug one but you have filled it up again.' Gaunt re-opened the grave but Bridgwater filled it in, then took a spadeful of earth aiming at Gaunt's face, but hitting him on the legs and thigh and causing the blood to flow. Shortly afterwards the funeral procession arrived, the vicar of Clent and Rowley, the Rev. John Perry, officiating. He said to Bridgwater, 'What is the cause of all this? You interrupt me in my office.' The relevant page in the register has been partly torn out, so there is no way we can tell whose funeral it was, but we may suspect that the quarrel went deeper than appears. Daniel Bridgwater is recorded as being cantankerous: when he died in 1795 it was noted that he had not spoken to his wife for many years until just before his death.

Richard Gaunt's school seems to have been the only one in Rowley parish at this time. He claimed to be receiving £10 per annum from Lady Monins' charity, paid by the then proprietors of Derrett's Hall. For this sum he educated 24 children for free in addition to the paying pupils. He had set up as a schoolmaster in about 1783, but retained his function as parish clerk. The Gaunt family seems to have been energetic and resourceful. Richard's wife and daughter Hannah helped in the school; his brother Tycho became a surgeon in Birmingham and features in one of the few surviving monuments from those times in Rowley church. Descendants still live in the area.

V

# Beginnings of the Industrial Revolution

The end of Rowley as a pastoral community was near, for the whole of the West Midlands would soon be transformed into a hive of industry, 'the workshop of the world'. To this workshop, Rowley would contribute iron ore, stone and coal. Industry in Birmingham and Wolverhampton was intensifying by the late 1760s and transport became an increasing problem. Loads of coal and iron bars were hard to move by packhorse, and the need to carry bulk cargoes was solved by the arrival of canals, huge engineering projects the like of which had not been seen in the Black Country before. Surveys for the canal from Birmingham to Wolverhampton began in 1767. It cut through Tividale, entering the parish at Brades Farm, then running under the turnpike road past the front of Derrett's Hall, after which it left the parish for Tipton. Along its banks various works were soon located. Within the next few years Brades steelworks was built, and by 1800 this had steam engines, forges, shops and workmen's

50 *The Spring House, Springfield, later the* Royal Oak *public house.*

JOHN Son of Jeremiah and Mary Gaunt
died 24ᵗʰ October 1777 aged 63
ALICE his Wife died 18ᵗʰ August 1783
Aged 69
TYCHO Their Son
lately of Birmingham Surgeon
died 2ⁿᵈ June 1814 Aged 74
Erected by the Executors of the Same
Tycho Gaunt December 1814

51    *Memorial to the Gaunt family in Rowley church which was originally in the first church.*

houses. The deep coal mine opened at Tivi-dale in 1794 by James Keir may be the first anywhere in Rowley parish. Thomas Telford shortened the canal route by about seven miles in 1838.

By 1793 it had become clear that a second canal would be needed. Known as the Dudley No. 2 Canal, it was to connect Windmill End and Netherton with Halesowen and the Worcester Canal at Selly Oak in the parish of Northfield, and provided an alternative route to Birmingham. It involved Irish navvies digging two tunnels, one in Rowley parish and one in Halesowen and Northfield. The first burrowed under Gorsty Hill from Slack Hillock (Station Road, Old Hill) to Coombs Wood, while the second, called the Lapal Tunnel, ran under parts of Halesowen and Woodgate to emerge at California near Weoley Castle. It was nearly 3,500 yards long. The tunnels were very narrow and a timetable had to be produced so that boats passed through in one direction for a certain number of hours, then the other way for a certain period. Dudley No. 2 Canal was begun in 1794 and opened in 1798.

The main industrial development in Rowley Village was in quarrying. This meant

providing more housing for workmen and the Rowley Regis Building Society was formed in about 1794 to cater for this need. The society sold shares in the enterprise, which was speculative, the entrepreneurs not intending to live in the houses themselves. A meeting was held to decide how many houses to build and it was agreed to begin with four; plans were drawn up by John Mackmillan and wells were dug. Bricks were bought at 18s. per thousand, and Joseph Edwards, James Ingley, John Bissell and John Auden agreed with Jesse Taylor to build the houses, each with a nailshop and a 'necessary house' to be finished by 10 June 1795. By 1797 the number of houses had increased to eight, and at least three tenants had moved in by 1800. The Club Buildings, on the site of Stanford Road, lasted until the 1960s.

Stebbing Shaw, the Staffordshire histor-ian, seems to have paid a visit to Rowley in preparation for his county history, published in 1798. He was far from delighted by what he found. The church has fabric that is 'the least of anything remarkable that I ever saw'. He noted that patching of the original stonework had been done with brick, which he thought surprising in view of the abundance of rag-stone in the vicinity. The reason may have been the difficulty of working local stone to precise sizes. He noted a Gothic 'niche' in the church which had been used for holy water, and a flat white marble stone on which only three letters were still visible. Unfortunately he fails to tell us what they were, but we may remember the will of William Orme, who desired to be buried 'in the Churche of Rowley under the marble stone' at his death in 1611. Perhaps there never were more than three letters, ORM, or at most the name 'Orme'. Vaults in churches are frequently marked with the surname only. No one could inform Shaw 'to what person or family belonged the dumb and useless memorial'. This was not the Haden memorial, which we know to have been of brass. Shaw then went outside the church and discovered an open 'charnel grave' on the north side, where he saw a great number of human skulls and bones, presumably those of paupers and others who could not pay for a proper burial.

**52** *The Club Buildings, on the site of Stanford Drive.*

**53** *Old cottages on the corner of Mackmillan Road, Blackheath.*

54  *Corngreaves Hall, home of the Attwood family, in July 1960.*

So-called 'waste', heath and moorland, was prominent in Rowley parish. There were large tracts at Cradley Heath and Blackheath, and the major landholders decided to promote an Enclosure Bill which went forward in 1799, resulting in an Act and Award in 1807-8. Its effect was to parcel out about 300 acres of common pasture in 228 separate holdings and to commute some ancient manorial duties and rights in both manors. The 'tithes' – contributions to the church from tenants and landowners – were also commuted. Among the duties to the church which seem to have been lost were the levies of 4d. for each man or maidservant, 2d. for each 'day's math' (three-quarters of an acre) of hay and 2d. for each peck of hemp or flax sown.

The Enclosure Award named the lords of the two manors as William Viscount Dudley and Ward (Rowley Regis) and Granville Leveson Gower, Marquis of Stafford (Rowley Somery). The Rev. Lyttelton Perry, Vicar of Clent, would be compensated for loss of tithes by 11 acres additional glebe land at Cradley Heath and about 39 acres at Blackheath. The Regis manor was so much larger than the Somery one that most of the allocations were made to the Regis proprietors. Among freeholds relieved of manorial dues were those of James Attwood, including Bearmore Coppice Farm, Smart's Meadow and Corngreaves; John Beet, the Hall Farm (Rowley Hall); Thomas Holbeche, Warren's Hall; William Hunt, the Brades; John Haden, Hayseech, The Moors and other land at, for example, Beauty Bank; James Keir and Alexander Blair, Tividale Hall; the Marquis of Stafford, the Old Fields at Old Hill.

Existing landholders could also attend the auction where they could buy land adjoining their own property. James Attwood, ironmaster, bought land near Corngreaves; John Allden, blacksmith, land at Gorsty Hill; John Beet, who gave his occupation as 'butcher', land at Whiteheath; Richard Bate, farmer, land at Tippity Green; Isaac Downing, nailer, land at Turner's Hill; Richard Gaunt, land at Portway Hall; Stephen Rollinson, butcher, land at Reddal Hill; and Thomas Sidaway, also land at Reddal Hill. The list includes many more and gives a fair idea of the names of influential inhabitants of Rowley at the start of the 19th century.

The effect of these changes was to clear the way for the expansion of industrial activity on a large scale. In particular, the extra land at Corngreaves was to be used by the Attwoods and their successors for the development of their ironworks; enclosures near the Brades allowed expansion of the steel mills. Quarrying and coal mining could also expand, and the new glebe land would eventually provide the capital for a new parish church. Of all the purchasers of land and those allotted it, only James Purser lived at a distance, in London; all the rest were resident in the locality, many actually in Rowley parish.

55 *Houses in Beauty Bank, Old Hill.*

56  *George Barrs, reforming curate of Rowley Regis.*

In 1800 a new and energetic curate was appointed to Rowley church: George Barrs was to be one of the major forces for change in the parish for the next forty years. Born near Nuneaton, he would make his home at Haden Hill, marrying the widow of John Haden and administering the parish as much from that house as from the vestry. It may have been his arrival that caused the parish map to be made, surveying the parish for tax purposes and also providing our earliest complete picture of the area. From the first Barrs took a studied interest in the habits and characteristics of his parishioners, recording some of their foibles in the parish register. He also recorded details of the old church, and fought desperately for a replacement.

Barrs' comments on the parish dead begin in 1800. On 29 January he buried 'a youth … killed by the swivel bridge over

57  *Graves of Thomas Cooksey and Thomas Wright in Rowley churchyard. Note the ornate carving.*

58   *St Luke's churchyard, Cradley Heath, with the former United Counties Bank.*

the canal at the Brades'. On 29 March he records the death of Joseph Windsor, 'who lived like an infidel, but yet was some years governor of the workhouse'. (The workhouse was on the south side of the road to Pensnett, just beyond Tippity Green.) Alice Rolinson was buried in 1802, murdered by a hot nail rod which driven into her side penetrated her liver. A coroner's court passed a verdict of wilful murder, but the alleged murderer was acquitted. In February of the following year David Parsons died at Bilston and his body was returned to Rowley, where he had lived. He had been taken to Bilston 'raving mad' and had continued there for a year, still raving, but no one knew why this was.

In May Mary Foxall was asleep near her fire when sparks landed on her clothes and set them alight. This woke her up and she ran out of the house, but was so badly burnt that she could not move any further. In October a boy named Henry Edmunds was killed in a coal pit at Brierley Hill. His clothes caught on the hook of a skep and he was dragged up the mine shaft, hanging on by his clothes. These tore and he clung on with his fingers, but eventually he could hang on no longer, and fell and 'spoke no more'. The wife of Daniel Johnson, who lived at Portway, was a 'thoughtless woman' who made a boast that she would outlive her son, William Eagles Johnson. She was suddenly taken ill and died within 12 hours. In January 1805 a hearty and active 84-year-old, Edward Round, left home at about 10 in the morning to walk along the road to Langley. His neighbours saw him walking with 'speed and sprightliness', but he was found dead before 12 on the road by Titford Bridge: 'His soul had winged her way into eternity.'

**59**  *The* Barley Mow, *Upper Tividale, photographed in 1962.*

John Homer died in February 1807. He was walking what is now called Dudley Road, between the *Cock* tavern 'at Cock Green' and the workhouse, when the innkeeper saw him fall and went to help. He pulled Homer to his feet, but Homer collapsed again. The innkeeper pulled him up and began to walk him along the road towards the workhouse, but he died at once. As well as fire and the dark canal waters, drunkenness appears to have been a frequent cause of death. 'Let every drunkard beware,' says George Barrs, recording the death of Joseph Hackett, who spent every penny he got on ale except for a very small portion which he spent on food. He left an alehouse on Christmas night after spending the whole day there 'in a state of intoxication, uttering profane curses'. He was discovered on Boxing Day morning, 'dead and cold at a very small distance' from the public house.

# VI

# Administrative Collapse

As industrialisation developed, methods of administering village communities like Rowley failed to cope with its effects. In 1800 there was no one to organise sewerage, water supply, health or planning. Road mending, land taxing, poor relief, care of the newborn and dying, education, all were the responsibility of Rowley parish church, which administered these matters throughout the chapelry, with the minimal help of turnpike trusts for two roads, an education foundation for two small schools, and charity. A committee called the Vestry met from 1798 'to consult … on a Method to repair the Road (the same being under an indictment) leading from Gorsty Hill to … Whiteheath':

> Agreed that the same shall be put in good and substantial repair as soon as maybe if the Weather permits So that the same may be completed by the later End of July next … Likewise agreed that John Mackmillan and Thomas Sidaway have the Superattendance & to see the same done & that the Expenses be defray'd them by the Overseers of the Poor out of the poor Rates for the Time being …

It is clear that this road would take some time and be difficult to get into good shape.

Later, the parish bought two iron scrapers, four round pointed shovels, a lock with a hollow in the middle and a hole for the stones to be driven through, a block and ring for breaking stones, and a hand hammer. A stamp with R.REGIS was bought to mark iron belonging to the parish, theft being a major concern.

When George Barrs took over, he must have felt the magnitude of the task facing him. But Barrs was a spirited fighter, and prepared to take on busybodies and idlers alike. He left us a description of the medieval church and its various inappropriate modifications (which will be dealt with in a later chapter), and the story of his first 12 years was that of his struggle to have the church replaced.

In 1808 a committee of five was set up to find architects to provide two estimates, one for repairing the church, and one for demolishing it and building a new one. In October it reported that the present church could not be enlarged for much less than the cost of a new one, and a plan was carried forward to 1809 for a new church, using either bricks at 32s. per thousand or 'Wheely [Weoley] Castle stone', which would be transported by the new canal from the ruins of the castle through the Lapal tunnel and under Gorsty Hill.

Another committee sought the appropriate people to 'farm' the poor. It was eventually decided that Edward Giles of Birmingham should have the contract at the cost of £1,050

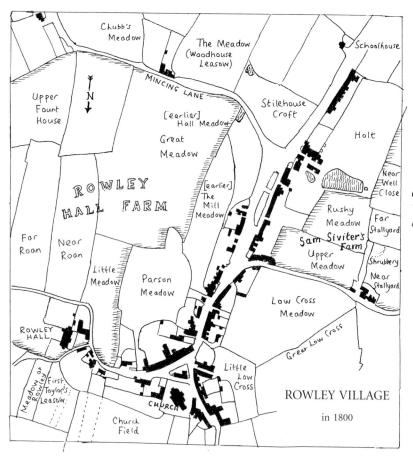

**60** *Map of Rowley Village in 1800, based on the parish plan.*

per annum. The parish overseers were to pro-vide 'proper Furniture Utensils and Bedding & Bed Clothes'; the poor house was to be put in good repair and new rooms built for Mr Giles to live in.

At the end of 1809 'the Honourable Mr Shirley', acting for Lord Dudley, was to solicit subscriptions from an interesting list of important landowners and industrialists in the neighbourhood. Only three of these gentle-men agreed to pay: the Marquis of Stafford (100 guineas), the Bishop of Worcester (£50) and Thomas Hill (£20). By 1810 an alternative plan, to modify the existing church, had been suggested. An Act of Parliament would be needed if the whole church were replaced, and a meeting of inhabitants was called.

Only 15 turned up. An alternative meeting was held in Dudley which championed the repairing option. A counter-meeting was called at Rowley that declared the Dudley meeting 'in no respect sanctioned', and was this time attended by 83 inhabitants. However, by March 1812 Mr Benjamin Wyatt of Sutton Coldfield was engaged to see if the church could be enlarged rather than a new one built. After four years' wrangling, the position had not changed and the issue was to rumble on for almost another thirty years.

There was no regular police force at this time. It was for the Church Vestry to try to sort out problems resulting from bad behaviour at public houses. James Nock, for example, allowed tippling on a Sunday at his pub at Reddal Hill, and set up a bowling alley in the public highway. Mrs Nock was asked to stop it and replied 'with great impertinence' that it was allowed in Dudley and she didn't see why it shouldn't be in this parish. Joshua Flavell allowed a bull to be baited at his pub in Slack Hillock 'to the terror and disturbance of the neighbourhood', and when asked to stop he said 'he should do as he liked'. The meeting opposed any further licensing of premises in the parish as they were 'already sufficiently numerous'.

Meanwhile, John Attwood of Corngreaves dug a hole in Pig Lane (Barrs Road) for use as a sawpit. It was resolved at a meeting of the Vestry on 13 July 1825 that he should be prosecuted at the assizes at the cost of the parish, because he had also cut down trees, laid down a 'railroad' and installed a weighbridge. One particular cause of danger, in the view of the Vestry, was the way this railroad did not follow the exact line of the road, but was raised or lowered according to the contours in such a way as to hinder travellers along Pig Lane. Attwood was not the only offender,

but the Vestry hoped to make an example of him, and gave notice to others creating a nuisance in any of the highways to 'remove such nuisance without delay'. This appears to be the first written evidence for the building of a mineral line in Rowley.

One reason for the lawlessness evident in these examples was perhaps the lack of any clear authority. Rowley Hall had been neglected for many years and there was no 'squire'. When Mary Grove married Francis Eld on 20 May 1703 the ownership of the hall was vested in a family of London-based lawyers. To begin with the Elds baptised their children at Rowley church, but this practice ceased as the emphasis moved to London. Francis Eld, described as of the Middle Temple, died in 1760, leaving the Hall to relatives who, as far as we know, did not even visit Rowley. By the beginning of the 19th century the old Hall must have become decrepit; before 1808 it was bought by John Beet, a Birmingham manufacturer. He totally rebuilt it, moving it onto an adjacent site.

**61**  *The Hailstone in 1845, with Hailstone Farm in the distance.*

It has been said that the Gunpowder Plotters hid in the cellars of what became Rowley Hall Farm. However, comparison of the 1800 parish map, which shows the original location of the Hall, with the early OS maps shows that, as George Barrs says in his reminiscences, the new hall was not built on the foundations of the old. There is photographic evidence of a brick wall on a stone base which formed the boundary wall of a new enclosure. This stone foundation seems likely to have been the lowest courses of the east wall of the original Hall, but the last remnant of the medieval building was removed in the 1970s. John Beet turned the new Hall into a working farm, to which he brought his new wife Elizabeth after their marriage in 1815; his second wife, Mary Smith, whom he married in 1828, outlived him here and was still at this address at the time of the 1851 census. Beet died in 1844. He had not been a supporter of George Barrs in the plan to build a new church, his name never featuring on a list of parishioners attending meetings at this stage, but by 1822 he was a churchwarden and he later took part in the renewed efforts to rebuild the church. The new Rowley Hall was a redbrick Georgian gentleman's residence, but this was completely demolished in the 1970s.

In the 1820s and '30s the Vestry continued to struggle with the increasing population and effects of industrialisation. The New Poor Law required Rowley to join Dudley for poor relief provision; the parish petitioned against this, using the 1524 charter as a lever, but it did not win. Tenacious George Barrs began another attempt to rebuild the old church 'except the steeple [tower]', and this time proved successful, though he did not live to see the results of his labour. Vestry minutes are full of negotiations over finding ways to pay. A further issue was the terrible state of the roads, now needed for the transport of heavy loads of coal and stone; a new Act of Parliament was aimed at 'consolidating' the state of roads everywhere.

Another non-religious issue the Vestry had to tackle was roving mad dogs. In June 1827 the committee (George Barrs, Edward Bridgwater and George Thompson) determined that a notice be given 'to all persons to keep their dogs tied up'. Otherwise the dogs would be destroyed, and the owners made to pay 1s. for the privilege. Mr Robinson and Mr Dudley were to have the job of finding unmuzzled or untied dogs and destroying them. Much of the committee's time was spent discussing poor relief, provision of clothing for paupers, and making sure the able-bodied had working tools, as in the case of Joseph Whitehouse, whose landlord John Cole had 'distrained' them; Cole was to be prosecuted if he sold the tools.

Worse than all these issues was the cholera outbreak of 1832. The Vestry's chief method of fighting it was to whitewash houses with lime, if necessary providing the lime and a brush to do the job. But Rowley was lucky; spreading from lower lying Tipton (first case 15 June) and West Bromwich, cholera made little progress in the uplands of Turner's Hill and Rowley Village, where the water supply came from fresh springs. Fifty-two people did die in the parish, and the attack of the disease was so sudden that mourners at a funeral one day would be buried themselves the next, but the percentage of deaths was small compared with the neighbouring areas to the north. The last case was reported in Dudley on 29 November 1832, but the epidemic forced the government to think about public health in the congested new industrial areas of the Midlands and North, and eventually Local Boards of Health were introduced.

# VII

# Heavy Industry

With the opening of the canals at each side of the hill range, the stage was set for industrial expansion. The first coal pit on the Old Hill side was at Totnal Moor ('The Old Lion') where we learn from the register that 'pious Christian James Hill' was killed by a fall of earth in January 1796. Coal was transported from here along the Dudley No. 2 canal via a specially built wharf. Another early pit was the 'Black Waggon', but soon there were a number of pits in Old Hill, some owned by the Haden family, George Barrs included. By 1821 pits had also been opened at The Knowle and at Cradley Heath. The earliest pit in Tividale was opened in 1794

to serve the ironworks of Keir and Blair at Bloomfield, Tipton, and later connected to the works by a mineral railway. Keir's Bridge was named after James Keir, who had built his alkali works at Tipton in 1780. By 1860 the following coalmasters were to be found at Rowley Regis: T. & I. Badger, Old Hill; J. Bennett, Blackheath; S. Bradley, Tividale; Joseph Darby, Rowley Village; William Dawes, Portway Hall; G. Dudley, Whitehall (Cradley Heath); J. Hackett, Blackheath; Hall, Holcroft & Pearson, Ash Tree (Old Hill); Hickman & Wright, Old Hill Colliery; J. G. Higgs, Eagle Colliery (across Totnal Bridge); Hopkins & Bradley, Tividale Hall; King, Swindells & Evers,

**62** *Chattock's engraving of 'The Gin'.*

Cradley Heath; S.Nicklin, Rowley Village; Nock, Wood & Nock, Burn Hill; Robert Poole, Hyatts Colliery; Round Brothers, Tividale; A. Sparrow, Cradley Heath; Swindell & Collis, Granville Colliery, High Haden; J. Thompson, Knowle; Waldren & Skidmore, Old Hill.

In the 1831 census 7,438 inhabitants are recorded in Rowley parish, many of whom were involved in mining or steelmaking. Shortly afterwards it was reported that the British Iron Company had the most extensive iron and steel works at Corngreaves, and Samuel Evers a large bar iron manufactory at Cradley Heath. Benjamin Best was the agent for the iron company. At the Brades Thomas Hunt carried on a family business engaged in steel rolling. By now there were 38 beerhouses for workers to slake their thirst, and 27 slightly more respectable taverns. In an age when water might not be pure, ale was sometimes a safer drink and work in the furnaces was gruelling.

It is probable that a colliery at Brickhouse was typical of those being run. The estate was owned by Deritend chapel, Birmingham, in the parish of Aston, and the colliery leased by Joseph Fereday and John Jones of Windmill End, who had reckoned without the Russell's Hall fault which runs through Rowley parish. The surveyors reported that the terrain was 'very much thrown up and down by faults'. However, Fereday and Jones were not deterred, and in consequence went bankrupt in June 1829. The man who farmed land above the mine, Mr Levett, said that in 1841 coal was regularly coming out of the ground, but both weather and labour problems hampered production the following year. In 1843 it was reported that the surface of the ground was pitted and hollowed, allowing stagnant water to collect in the fields, because of broken drains and altered watercourses. The mineral rights had by this time passed to Samuel Danks of Wednesbury, who was also defeated by the terrain, as were his successors, the Withymoor Furnace Co. The mine was then bought by a Mr Mills, proprietor of Gawne colliery, who successfully worked three acres of it until he too went bankrupt, in 1868, and the mine passed to Noah Hingley of

63   *Chattock's engraving of Timbertree Colliery in the 19th century.*

**64**   *Waterfall Lane pumping station, showing Old Hill station and the Dudley branch.*

**65**   *The Black Waggon pit in the 19th century, part of the Corngreaves empire.*

**66** *Miners at work in Saltwells Colliery (just outside Rowley Regis). From Griffiths'* Guide to the Iron Trade of Great Britain.

the Netherton steelworks. The last serious attempt to work Brickhouse colliery was in 1881. This, too, failed and the mine was left derelict and flooded, the result of a failure on

**Cinder Bank Gate**

Frees Wilkes Fold, Old Hill, Netherton. Grange, Coombes, Cinder Bank, and Manor Lane gates and bars.

day                Mo.        187

**Produce the ticket or pay the toll.**

**Bumble Hole Gate,**

Frees Tansley Hill, Dixon's Green, Tipperty Green, & Long Lane Gates & Bars.

day                        Mo 186

**Produce the Ticket or Pay the Toll.**

*67  Turnpike gate tickets.*

the part of the mine owners of the district to combine on any form of corporate drainage system. Clearly, money was made from coal mining, yet the methods of prospecting and sinking pits were very unscientific, and coal exploitation could be very 'hit and miss'.

The idea was to work the coal and other minerals such as iron and fireclay at the same time, leaving pillars to support the roof, then work over a second time, removing the pillars. Fire often broke out and underground fires continued to burn in places such as Netherton churchyard for many years. At Brickhouse the entrance to one of the shafts was through highly combustible thick coal, which was obviously a recipe for fires. Buildings above the mines began to slip and sag, the most august of these being the parish church itself. Mr Job Taylor, mining engineer, was eating breakfast at Portway Hall one morning in 1837 when the mine underneath moved and caused the ceiling to fall in on him. Brickhouse may have been a particularly unfortunate colliery, and there are many examples of financial as well as personal disaster in the Rowley coal industry. The greatest loss of all was to

**68** *The* Titanic *anchor leaves Hingley's works (from* A Brief Intimate Story of Netherton and St Andrew's Church*).*

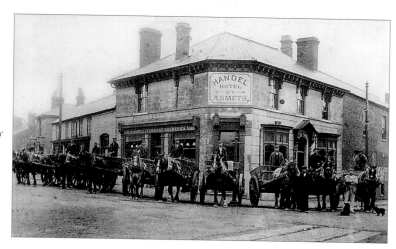

**69** *The* Handel Hotel, *Blackheath, on the corner of Oldbury Road.*

**70** *The* Bull's Head, Tippity Green, *now called* The Chaplin. *The outhouses were formerly a small brewery.*

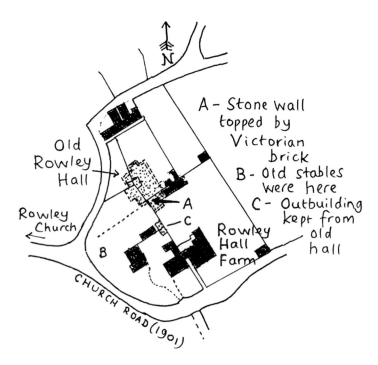

A – Stone wall topped by Victorian brick
B – Old stables were here
C – Outbuilding kept from old hall

Old Rowley Hall

Rowley Church

Rowley Hall Farm

CHURCH ROAD (1901)

*71   Plan of Rowley Hall, showing location of the original Hall and the Hall Farm built in the early 19th century.*

the landscape itself, which was completely changed by the extraction of coal. While the ground sagged, pit banks grew everywhere, overshadowing the scene in a way that is now impossible to imagine. Almost all have been levelled and had houses built on them; just one or two, for example at Haden Hill and Warren's Hall, have been covered with trees and form interesting landscape features.

In the Black Country almost all of the underground work was done by men, while boys would do light jobs such as holding lamps and candles. The women worked above ground as 'pit bank girls' and a magazine article of 1863 describes them as having 'an air of robust health'. Their jobs included taking charge of the 'skips' bringing up the coal and ironstone from the mine and delivering them to the banks. The women then sorted the iron from the coal, removed shale and piled the iron ore in quadrangular heaps to be washed by the rain. The article comments that these

girls are dressed shabbily on weekdays, but on a Sunday (even though not at church) they are clean and have bright complexions, shining eyes and clothes which are cheap but dressy. Underground was a system of railway tracks, metal hoppers being pulled at the early stage by pit ponies; some steam engines were introduced later.

Small farmers were still trying to make a living on the surface above the coal pits. At Brickhouse successive farmers followed Mr Levett in trying to cope with the poor drainage and growing spoil heaps; these encouraged weeds and leached harmful acids into the soil. Fences and gates were broken and this encouraged trespassing, so that crops would be trampled by colliers taking short cuts to their work. It was believed that potatoes could be a profitable crop, but they did not succeed. In 1869 William Davis tried to run sheep on Brickhouse, but he was at the end of his resources and even the farm

72 'Cobbs' engine house. No one called Cobb is traceable, and the name may be a corruption of 'copyhold'.

73 Tividale aqueduct (also called Groveland aqueduct) took the Brindley Canal over the Netherton Branch.

74  *A quiet stretch of Dudley Canal No. 2, at Old Hill.*

75  *The* Boat *public house, Station Road, Old Hill, in 1970.*

buildings leaked water. The value of the farm sank from £150 in 1830 to £75 and it must have been a similar story for many a farm in Rowley.

At the time of the Enclosure Award in 1806 much of the area round Corngreaves in Cradley Heath was in the hands of Matthew Attwood of Corngreaves Hall. On this site was built a vast enterprise producing iron and steel, the biggest in the Black Country. It would include rivet and boiler shops, chain works, a sawmill, brickworks and other plants. The problems faced by George Barrs with respect to the sawpit and railway on Pig Lane were doubtless due to this work. Meanwhile, in the west of the parish, straddling the border with Netherton, Sir Horace St Paul built another iron works, and across on the Tipton border stood Hunt's Brades steel works. These added to the effects of coal mining in changing the face of Rowley Regis.

Corngreaves iron works were owned by the British Iron Company and subsequently by the New British Iron Company. A jubilee brochure contains an impression of the works in their early days in 1825, a small enterprise with one major building, but by mid-century the hissing steam and noise of hammering echoed throughout the valley, the vegetation drooped under the layers of coal and clay dust which issued in clouds from works and railway tracks. In 1860 James Hunt was the general manager at Corngreaves and the works manufactured pig iron, bars, rods, hoops, plates and shuts. As well as these assets the company owned 560 acres of minerals below ground (though this total includes assets in neighbouring parishes). Surface leases generally excluded mineral rights, which went to mining and iron companies, who were thus able to exploit the mines without reference to the damage they may

76   *The pedestrian bridge at Warren's Hall, made at Toll End works, Tipton.*

*77    Former Lion tube works, Waterfall Lane, Old Hill on a quiet day in autumn 1970.*

have been causing above ground through pollution and subsidence.

In April 1863 a standard gauge freight line was built by the GWR to link Corngreaves with its line to Stourbridge, opened at the same time. Remarkably, this remained open until 12 January 1965 despite the closure of Corngreaves. Work at the factory was hazardous. In 1867 a tuyere (the nozzle through which the blast is delivered to the furnace) shattered and allowed water to meet with the molten metal. The resulting steam scalded three furnacemen and killed 44-year-old Benjamin Hodgetts and William Kilvert. An

anxious crowd gathered outside the works, but a local newspaper described the management at Corngreaves as 'excellent' and the firm claimed the equipment had been examined that morning. The coroner recorded verdicts of accidental death.

There were other accidents in this complex, including a major one in 1887. By this time, however, the threat of bankruptcy was hanging over the New British Iron Company, following the 'Great Depression' which was at its worst in 1879. The end came in 1893, when Corngreaves was put up for sale at the *Queen's Hotel*, Birmingham.

As well as the ironworks and blast furnaces, mills, forges and manufactories of small items such as rivets, the company owned winding, pumping and hauling engines in the colliery section, and miles of mineral lines. Corngreaves Hall, the Gothic-style mansion of the Attwoods, formed part of the assets. 'Intellectual property' in the form of trade marks was also up for sale. A viable purchaser was found in the shape of Corngreaves Furnace Company, which scaled down the works (the old works closed on 31 July 1894) and, under the management of Robert Fellows, ordered modern equipment, including new steam locomotives to haul the mineral trucks. The blast furnaces continued to work until 1912.

At the Tividale end of the parish Brades steel works was known by 1835 as William Hunt and Sons (The Brades) Ltd. Other members of the family, Thomas and his sons, owned local coal mines. One of the best contemporary accounts of the works is given in Elihu Burritt's book *Walks in the Black Country and its Green Borderland*, published in 1868. Exaggerating a little, the American pro-consul claimed that the works had been in existence for more than a century. Mentioning first the seven coal pits owned by the company, he stands amazed at the huge power and size of the enterprise and watches the iron ore worked into pigs and then into iron bars which are then taken to the carbonising kilns where the iron is saturated with carbon fumes. After this, much of the iron was broken up again for melting in the blast furnaces, of which the Brades had about twenty.

78    *The north entrance to the Netherton Tunnel in March 1960.*

Burritt watched the lids being removed and was almost blinded by the searing light. He saw the men, naked to the waist, pouring the fervid fluid into flasks to make ingots of cast steel, still supple enough when somewhat cooled to be hammered and rolled into all sorts of shapes and sizes. From this agricultural tools were made, but Brades also supplied the Birmingham pen trade up to about 1850. A major export was plantation tools for the American and Brazilian cultivation of cotton. Brades also made shovels, spades, garden hoes, mould boards for ploughs and many other pieces of steel equipment. 'One cannot contemplate their operations and productions without admiration', remarks Elihu Burritt, yet within less than twenty years his own nation's production would begin to outstrip the Black Country.

Victorian government became anxious about the state of workers in industry and their reports are full of information and impressions of industrial towns. In 1863 reporters said of the Black Country iron workers,

[They] have warm feelings, and show great kindness to each other in times of difficulty and distress. In one poor-looking cottage, perhaps, may be found an orphan child, adopted by a kind neighbour, on whom it has no claim but its helplessness; in another a poor woman, whose sick husband is occupying their only bed, and who has been taken in by a kind friend for her approaching confinement.

One major abuse was the existence of 'tommy shops'. Iron and steel masters would set up shops to sell provisions or clothing where the workers had to go to spend their wages, sometimes given in the form of trade tokens instead of coinage. Though this could occasionally work to the benefit of the employees, since through bulk purchase the owner could actually provide commodities more cheaply, more often the employers made profits from the system. A case was reported of a wagoner charged 17s. 6d. for a 5s. pair of trousers. An Act of Parliament was passed in 1821 to outlaw this system, but in 1860 the writer Walter White reported that it still existed in the area round Tipton.

# VIII

# Quarrying and Brick Making

The mineral wealth of the parish was by no means confined to coal and ironstone. As the industrial revolution took hold there was more and more demand for building materials, brick and stone. The dolerite of which Turner's Hill is composed had been used for making walls and small buildings for many years. There have been examples throughout Rowley Village down the ages, such as the house in Siviter's Lane from 1663, the inventory of 1591 mentioning 'blowe stone' and the churchyard being 'fenced' with a stone wall in 1661. But the local stone was always difficult to work and in 1709 the new porch for the church was 'new built from the ground with good brick'. We cannot be sure when Brickhouse received its name, and it may signify 'not wood' rather than 'not stone' anyway. Boundary walls on Turner's Hill were formerly of stone, and there are numerous examples of stone walls still remaining, but these may be from the 18th or 19th centuries.

The earliest quarrying may well have been near the church, perhaps at Tippity Green (later called Allsop's Hill), but two

79   *The* Neptune *at Old Hill, on the canal bank.*

63

80  *An impression of brickyard 'pages' at work.*

81  *Corngreaves Iron Works – an interpretation of the souvenir picture of 1885.*

other early sites seem to have been on the south side of Portway Hill and near the hailstone, a strange rock formation near the Knowle still remembered in the name of *The Hailstone* public house. In the 17th century Dr Plot suggested that it might have been made by humans, but later historians thought this ridiculous. In Garner's *Natural History of the County of Stafford* (1845) Rowley stone is described as 'trap'. Garner mentions its local name, Rowley rag, and says that by his time this 'hard, fine grained, crystalline greenstone' was much quarried for road making, though Shaw (1798) calls it 'a rusty blue'. Garner evidently visited the Pearl Quarry, where he noted the 'columnar form' of the strata, already observed in an article for *The Gentleman's Magazine* in 1812.

Directories in 1834 and 1835 do not mention quarrying as a trade. However, by 1860 there is a 'farmer and quarryman' at Hailstone Farm. From this it may be fair to deduce that quarrying was initially carried on as an adjunct to farming, and on a very small scale. But an advertisement of 1860 claims that Frost Brothers of Tividale Stone Quarry can supply stone 'superior to any other in Staffordshire for paving and Macadamising purposes … in any quantities', so it is surprising that they are absent from the classified directory. The hailstone itself was destroyed as part of a quarrying operation in 1879, two workmen, Fred Wright and Benjamin Bate, also being killed. At the end of the 19th century there were quarries at Darby's Hill, Lye Cross, Rough Hill, Hailstone (its stone now taken by inclined railway to the canal basin near Dog Lane bridge), Higham's Hill, Church Hill, Allsop's Hill, Prospect (behind Hawes Lane), Rowley Hall, Portway and elsewhere. In the early years of the 20th century the Hailstone quarry was owned by Rowley Regis Granite Company, while those on the other side of Turner's Hill were the property of the Richards brothers.

There are many 19th-century accounts of the working of brickyards. Unlike the quarries, these were not localised in the higher parts of the parish but were found all over the region, though Rowley certainly had its fair share. Factory inspectors sent in reports about the brickmakers' illiteracy and immorality, noting that women workers mixed on flippant and familiar terms with the men and boys, and frequently produced illegitimate children: 'Clad in a few dirty rags, their bare legs exposed far above the knee, their hair and faces covered with mud, they learn to treat with contempt all feelings of modesty and decency.'

Elihu Burritt visited the brickworks near Old Hill station for his *Walks in the Black Country* and his description is most detailed and evocative. He first watched the clay, enough for 500 bricks at a time, being moved from the clay pit by a steam engine and an inclined tramway. He noted the kilns, heated to a temperature similar to that needed for

82 *The new Haden Hill House, built in the 19th century.*

iron production, and the long kneading sheds in which the workers, mainly women, shaped the clay. He watched one woman, drenched in sodden clay, shaping bricks which he compared to loaves of bread. A small girl took

the wet brick and placed it in a regimental line of bricks waiting to be baked. Another, 'about thirteen', brought more clay. She would have been almost pretty, but though 'there was some colour in her cheeks' it was 'the

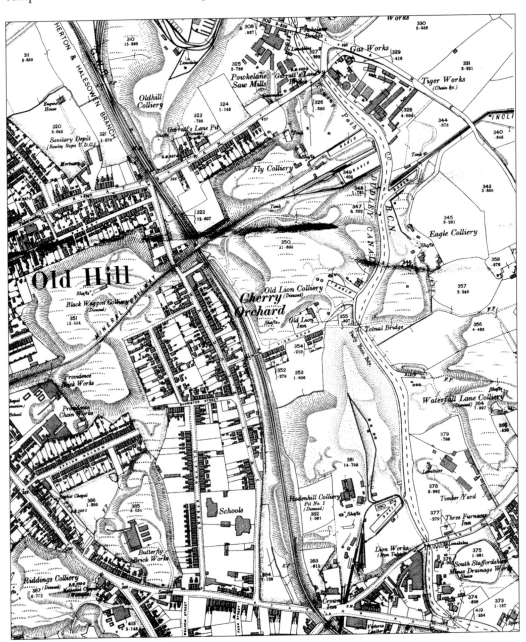

**83** *Map of Old Hill coal mines at the end of the 19th century.*

84  *Windmill End and Withymoor in the 19th century, looking towards Dudley.*

85  *Looking over old quarry sites at the rear of Hawes Lane. The former grammar school is on the left and the Clent Hills are in the distance.*

flitting flush of exhaustion'. The girl took a lump of clay weighing about 25 pounds on her head, squatted down and held another lump of the same size against her stomach with her hands then walked to the moulding bench to deposit the clay. Burritt was shocked at this kind of labour and not amused by the way the children were called 'pages' for the moulding woman. With two or three pages she could make 3,000 bricks a day, receiving 2s. 8d. per thousand and paying the pages 2s. per day or 8d. each.

86   *Rowley Regis
stone quarries.*

87   *A row of cottages
at Perry's Lake about
to be demolished.*

Burritt was told that the average hours for work were from 6 a.m. to 6 p.m. and the girls did not usually work overtime. The kilns were fired by men, who worked nights. The girls had even to come out on Sunday morning to turn the bricks made on the previous day. Much of this account supports the findings of another inspector, who noted that little work could be done when it was raining, so that in fine weather the girls worked from 6 in the morning till 9 at night, sometimes carrying four or five bricks; if they dropped them they could be smacked. The finished bricks were transported from Old Hill by the Great Western Railway at Old Hill sidings or by the Dudley No. 2 Canal. The proprietor, in his replies to Burritt's questions, seems to show that he has no conception of the women and children as fellow humans. He had no idea if any of the children could read, and congratulated himself that the new Factory Act concerning brick making would not affect him because it applied only to ornamental bricks.

Other Rowley workers were involved in the gun trade or in making jews' harps. The best known gun barrel works was at Hayseech, but the Barnsley family were also making guns at Newtown by 1835. The rather strange name of Ramrod Hall, at Whiteheath, is said to derive from the manufacture of steel ramrods in the area. One suggestion is that the builder of Ramrod Hall had made his fortune from those made at the Brades. Ramrod Hall seems to have been part of the Earl of Dudley's estate, and the chief occupation was certainly farming until the coal mine was developed. For a long while, at least from 1798 to 1835, the tenant farmer was Benjamin Hadley. The colliery was the scene of a serious accident in 1856 when 11 men died as the result of an explosion. It had

**88** *Quarryman's house at Perry's Lake.*

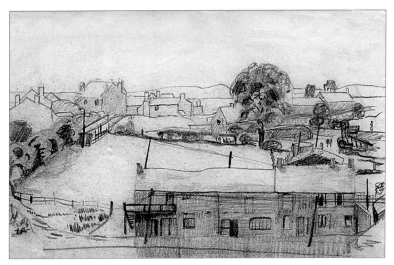

**89**  *The old quarry stables, drawn about 1960.*

been closed for four days and the disaster was the result of an inexperienced 'butty' (contracted-out supervisor) sending the men down without testing for fire-damp. The men detected the damp at once, and called for a lighted safety lamp, but the butty decided to bring a shovelful of fire down instead and immediately the explosion blew eight men to death in the descending skip (open lift) while three more died at the bottom of the shaft.

Jews' harps are said to be misnamed 'jaws' harps. They are shaped from a cut-out sheet of metal, with a protruding tongue used as a lever. The 'harp' fits between the player's teeth and is activated by striking the metal tongue with the finger, the note changing according to the force of the breath expelled. They were extremely cheap and popular in the mid-19th century and were exported from Rowley all over the world. Doubtless their manufacture developed from nailing. In the 1834 directory there are four makers of jews' harps, all in Rowley Village, who had been joined in 1835

by John Wakeman in Reddal Hill. During the next twenty years the manufacturing process became more industrialised and by 1860 production was concentrated in the works of George Gones of Blackheath and the Barnsleys of Cradley Heath.

Many individual manufacturers worked in associated trades, and mention should be made of Thomas Sidaway, a nail factor who also worked in tin-plating. He owned 'Reddall' Hill House, on the hill beyond the brook dividing Old Hill from Cradley Heath. (The parish vestry agreed in 1791 to rebuild the bridge over this brook – which they called a rivulet – and to level the banks on each side of the road.) Sidaway inherited the house built by his ancestor Benjamin Sidaway in 1759, and rebuilt it in grandiose style. Later it became the Liberal Club. Sidaway's name appears as churchwarden on the cast-iron safe in Rowley church vestry. But he was only one of many small manufacturers working in metal, principally as spin-offs from the nail and chain-making industries.

# IX

# Nail and Chain Making

Nail making was a major industry in Rowley from at least Tudor times. Wills from 1560 to 1729 contain the names of 70 nailers as testators, witnesses or beneficiaries, compared with 53 yeomen and 41 other trades such as bakers, tailors or scythe makers. This dominance does not cease in the early 19th century. The 1841 census Enumeration District 2, for example, covers part of Rowley Village, Ross and part of Blackheath, where about 130 adults in 173 houses describe themselves as nailers; and in Enumeration District 6, covering Windmill End, part of the Gawne and part of Old Hill, there are 127 nailers in 74 houses. (Comparisons cannot be exact, as there are differences in the way enumerators describe people, especially adolescents and older children.)

The hand-made nail trade was prevalent over a large part of south Staffordshire and north Worcestershire, including Dudley, West Bromwich, Oldbury, Halesowen, Quarry Bank, Northfield, Bromsgrove, Kingswinford and other places. Birmingham factories began to produce machine-made nails, making it harder for the home-workers to compete, but in earlier times the making of nails made up for poor agricultural returns and reduced the need for emigration from Rowley and district. A nailer's life was hard, but the work could be done at home, in the 'shop', and could involve quite young children. Compared with brick making, it provided a slightly more sheltered life for youngsters, and kept families together.

There were many different kinds of nails, and each nailer and his family made a specific type. They did not generally change. Horse nails were usually the province of male workers. In 1826 Thomas Pittaway of Blackheath listed his prices, ranging from brads at £9 2d. for 40lb to long horse nails at £6 11d. for 12lb. There were clasp nails, dog nails, tenter hooks, clench nails and many others. His reign as nail fogger (master and trader) does not seem to have lasted long; he was not a purchaser of land at the enclosure, and after the mid-1830s his name does not appear in directories.

Walter White visited Rowley for his book *All Round the Wrekin,* published in 1860. After noting the church 'as conspicuous from miles around as that of Harrow', he entered the village, with its characteristic 'click-click' and the thump of hammers: 'the whole village resounds with the strokes and each cottage has its little forge occupying the place of the wash-house'. Contrary to the suggestion of the 1841 census enumerator, who generally put down the head of the household as the nailer, in each shop were three or four women, assisted by children:

The fire is in common, and one after another giving a pull at the bellows, each woman beats the ends of two slender iron rods, withdraws the first, and by a few hammer strokes fashions and cuts off the nail, thrusts the end into the fire, and takes out the second rod, and gets a nail from that iron in the same way … 'It ain't work as pays for men' [says] one of the women 'and 'tain't much better than clemmin' for women.'

White visited another nail-shop, where the woman lamented that she could no longer start on Tuesday and earn 13 shillings a week. She had come to work the day after her baby had been born, since her husband was out of work. She then took out a tobacco pipe, 'to comfort herself'. White's description of this nailing family has the merit of being written at a time when the lives of few working people are on record.

A few years later Elihu Burritt walked from Old Hill to Halesowen, and spoke to a woman nailer whose husband was a collier who left her to carry on the nailing. She explained that she could only make nails four days a week, as she had to 'fettle' the house on the other day. She earned three or four shillings a week, not much but a great help in rearing her family. A seven-year-old girl entered the room. She had begun to read and her mother said she was determined her daughter should learn. Burritt says he enjoyed walking round nailing villages and he noted the way in which the architecture had been conformed to need, so that each house had its nail-shop. Nailers earned little, 'but they earn it at home'. The hill-top situations of the nailing villages made for healthier lives, he thought, comparing them with the 'better-paid mechanics in towns'. Here is one of the roots of the differing outlooks of people in some Black Country areas from those in the large cities of Wolverhampton and Birmingham.

However, depression was on its way and the factory-made nails were strong competition. J.E. White was commissioned to investigate conditions in the Birmingham metal manufacturing industries for a report published in 1864. While visiting a cottage

90   *A nailer at work.*

91 *A general view of Hayseech in the 1960s, showing the Methodist Chapel.*

in Halesowen he heard the sound of many voices: a crowd of men, women and children were singing a hymn and marching from 'villages near Dudley' to Halesowen, their aim being to get the Halesowen workers to join them in a strike. It was not clear whether Old Hill and Rowley would side with Dudley or Halesowen. A nailer told White that, though the work was healthy, it was a sweaty business, only tempered by the wind coming in at the window. Children were often ill and sometimes there were accidents like the one which had burned his little boy, when two small pieces of red-hot iron had dropped on to his leg. 'The scars are there now and always will be,' said the nailer.

In 1869 a reporter from the *Midland Industrial News* visited Old Hill to report on the eleven-week-old strike in the nailing industry. He interviewed William Wakeman, who said he could earn only eight shillings a week after paying for the nail rod, and of

this two shillings went in the house rent. George Parsons claimed to have earned 11 or 12 shillings a week, but he found it impossible to clothe his children. His living room had in it some tattered clothes hung up to dry after washing, a saucepan on the well-blacked hob, a tea-pot and one or two cups and a rough couch. Upstairs in the bedroom was one old bed with poor quality sheets, some sacking and a flock mattress. Five people had to sleep here: two parents, the son of 20, a girl of 15 and a small child of three. Their diet was tea and bread; they never had meat. The reporter summed up their poverty as being 'appalling in its intensity'.

Nearly twenty years after this the Board of Trade commissioned an enquiry into the work of nail and chain makers in the Black Country and it does not seem that much had changed. The commissioners reported that some women were now making large spike nails as big as six or seven inches and that

92  *Mushroom Green chain-shop, just inside Dudley.*

great power was needed to press down the pedal of the heavy oliver (the large hammer operated by foot treadle), which caused perspiration to pour down their cheeks. Unlike Burritt's informant, these women had no idea how to provide for their families in the most economical way. The investigator, much more censorious than those previously encountered, noted the untidiness of some of the homes, and commented on the sanitary inadequacy of the earth closets. He also felt that the women were working because the men took advantage of them to lead idle lives. The report of 1888 seems to see much of the same evidence as earlier ones, but to draw harsher conclusions.

Chain making was introduced to Rowley parish much later than nailing. Some attribute it to a visit by Noah Hingley to Liverpool, where the industry was well established, in about 1817. However, there does seem to be evidence of earlier chain making and undoubtedly this would have developed from the nail trade. By 1835 there were 14 chain makers in Dudley and Netherton, including Benjamin Hancox at Mushroom Green, just outside Rowley parish in Dudley Wood (called Mursham in the directory). Within Rowley the trade was almost entirely concentrated at Cradley Heath, with, at this date, nine manufacturers including five members of the Billingham family. Joseph Bannister and William Woodall give their place of work as Newtown, though three years later Bannister is at Lomey Town. Billinghams remained important workers and managers in the industry as long as it lasted. There may have been one or two more businesses engaged in the making of chain by 1835, since a few of those listed as 'Nail and Chain Manufacturers' are known to have specialised in chain. Among them was Daniel Grainger (also spelt 'Granger'), who lived at Grainger's Hall not far from the Five Ways. Two more chain makers were Charles and James Yardley, also at Cradley Heath.

The 1841 census shows chain making concentrated in Newtown, Tibbett's Gardens and Foxoak areas of Cradley Heath. It has not yet spread to Old Hill, where it was prominent by the turn of the 20th century. The establishment and spread of the hand-made chain industry seems to have been made possible by the decline in nail making since skills learned in the one could easily be transferred to the other. This may also account for the prominence of women in chain making, though they seem to have gradually taken on heavier work as the trade developed. The number of women involved in the role increased until in 1911 there were 2,103.

Typically, chains were made in small workshops not unlike the nail-shops they replaced and used the same methods: iron rods were collected by the outworker and returned when they were worked up. Many backyard chain-shops survived in various conditions right up to the middle of the 20th century and beyond. It was at Mushroom Green, however, just across the border, that it proved possible to bring back to life a most interesting example. This was due in great measure to the Black Country Society Industrial Archaeology Group led by Ron Moss. Their determination to save the near-derelict chain-shop eventually resulted in a working museum under the aegis of Dudley Borough. Mushroom Green grew from a tiny hamlet to a small village dedicated to the making of chain. It was dominated by the Kendrick family, who opened a six-hearth chain-shop in the late 1860s. Though the equipment from this shop had been dispersed, it proved possible to acquire various items from local chain-shops being dismantled in Old Hill and other places to set up a viable

museum, in which demonstrations take place each month. Like many houses in Old Hill, Cradley Heath and elsewhere, dwellings in Mushroom Green had to be pinned together by iron bars because of mining subsidence – in the case of Mushroom Green because of the Earl of Dudley's No.25 pit.

It was long thought impossible to make chain by welding, but when this was finally achieved it signalled the end of the Cradley Heath chain-shops. In order to compete, master chain makers cut or pegged wages, employing more and more women workers. This led inevitably to industrial unrest and just before the First World War a Wages Board was established, but master chain makers in some cases refused to pay. A strike which broke out in August 1910 lasted three months. Processions were organised by the secretary of the Women's Trade Union League, Mary Macarthur, and in the end the women, backed by the law, won the day.

93   *A wall from a half-timbered house used for a 19th-century cottage, photographed in 1960.*

Two very different women are remembered in connection with chain making in Old Hill and Cradley Heath. Eliza Tinsley took on the family business, making chains and cables as well as nails, rivets and anchors at the factory in Reddal Hill. The enterprise became known as Eliza Tinsley and Co. of Old Hill, and developed consistently before and after being sold in 1872. Eliza became a by-word for charity both in Old Hill and her home in Sedgley before dying in April 1882. Mrs Lucy Woodhall was known as the last chain maker in the old tradition working for Samuel Woodhouse & Sons Ltd for many years until her retirement in 1973. Three years later the local chain-making trade finished owing to a lack of wrought iron. For a while derelict chain-shops could be seen in Old Hill and Cradley Heath, and Ron Moss even reported one for sale in 1974, but most have now disappeared, leaving Mushroom Green to stand as a memorial to thousands of hours of labour and accurate craftsmanship.

# X

# Transport in Rowley

Transport was always likely to pose problems in the hilly chapelry and borough of Rowley Regis. For bulk transport of raw materials and manufactured goods out of the area, the canals had been constructed, but people needed increasingly to travel, since there was no local market, to neighbouring towns for trade and commerce. And as Rowley Village and church declined as the centre of social interaction, parts of the parish looked in different directions for a new centre: Cradley Heath and Old Hill needed good links to Dudley; Tividale became associated with Tipton and Oldbury; Blackheath required access to Birmingham.

The first main line railway, however, passed through Rowley without stopping: the LNWR line from Birmingham to Wolverhampton opened to passengers in 1852 but Dudley Port station was on the border of Grovelands, in Tipton. By 1860 it was seen that a route through Cradley Heath and Old Hill

**94** *Tram No. 196 in front of the* Boat *at Tividale.*

**95** *An old postcard of Cradley Heath High Street, showing the Dudley tram.*

**96** *A Midland Red timetable supplement for 1951.*

ASSOCIATED WITH
THE BRITISH ELECTRIC TRACTION CO LTD. AND
BRITISH RAILWAYS

## SEPTEMBER
## Supplement to
## TIME TABLES

Showing additions and alterations to
Time Table Book dated
**MAY, 5th, 1951**

Chief Offices :                                    D. M. SINCLAIR
BEARWOOD, BIRMINGHAM                                General Manager
            Telephone No : BEArwood 3030

*The friendly "Midland Red"*
**FREE ENTERPRISE AT YOUR SERVICE**

was necessary, and the Stourbridge Railway was incorporated to fulfil this purpose. The line reached Old Hill in 1866 and linked the area to Smethwick and Birmingham next year. Passengers could travel to either Snow Hill or New Street, and that is again the case today. The short branch to Corngreaves has already been mentioned, rail freight challenging and conquering the canals.

A less vital line was that from Halesowen to Dudley via Old Hill, which was opened in 1878, after considerable work building bridges, embankments and junctions. The centre of the line was Old Hill station, which now had rail links to the four points of the compass, and was to prove valuable after the extension to Northfield was built, providing quick transport to the Austin works at Longbridge when mining collapsed in the 1920s. The two other stations within the parish were 'Cradley Heath and Cradley' (from 1 July 1899) and 'Rowley Regis and Blackheath', both of which titles have now been appropriately shortened.

The branches from Old Hill to Dudley and Halesowen were not very successful, with competition from Midland Red buses, and the Halesowen service closed as early as 1927. A major blow was the report of Dr Beeching, who recommended in 1963 a drastic reduction in rail mileage. This led to the termination of the lines to Dudley and Longbridge and, more seriously, forced all lines in the Birmingham area into one major station at New Street. Stourbridge and Cradley

Heath trains were therefore re-routed, with inevitable congestion resulting, and Snow Hill station was demolished. The costly mistake was immediately regretted, and expensive measures were adopted to relay lifted track so that passenger services could resume. Eventually Cradley Heath (modernised in 1983) was reconnected to a new Snow Hill via a railway officially termed the 'Jewellery Line' since it runs through Birmingham's Jewellery Quarter.

Horse-drawn passenger trams began to be considered about 1870, and the Birmingham and District Tramways Co. Ltd was formed in 1871. Initially the purpose was to link Birmingham with places on the north side of the hill ridge, including Dudley Port, on the Tipton edge of Rowley. Many years would pass before Cradley Heath, Old Hill

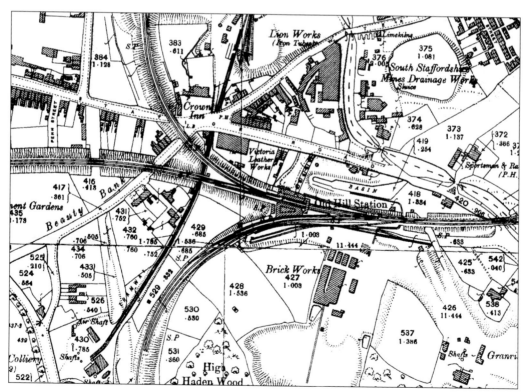

97   *Plan of Old Hill station.*

and Blackheath became part of a tramway system which never reached Rowley Village at all. However, Tividale was served by passenger trams in 1885. An interesting feature of Birmingham and Black Country tramways was the 3ft 6in gauge, which gradually became standard throughout the area, and can still be seen in operation at the Black Country Museum. It was, perhaps, this non-standard gauge which caused Birmingham and other local authorities to abandon trams in favour of buses and trolleybuses much earlier than other conurbations.

98 *The bus ticket shown on the far left is a Midland Red bus ticket before municipal reorganisation, the one on the right is a West Midlands bus ticket afterwards.*

99 *A page from the 'railway A to Z' showing the trains from Old Hill (High Street) and Windmill End with their connections to Birmingham (Snow Hill).*

G.W.R.] **HALESOWEN, GREAT BRIDGE, OLD HILL, OLDBURY, DUDLEY & BIRMINGHAM**

WEEK DAYS

| | SX am | am | am | am | SX a.m. | SX | SX am | am | am | am | am pm | a.m. | a.m. a.m. a.m. | p.m | S | S p.m | S pm pm pm pm |
|---|---|---|---|---|---|---|---|---|---|---|---|---|---|---|---|---|---|
| Dudley .......dp. | 558 | .. | 628 | 656 | 640 | .. | .. | 658 | 7 5 | 7 9 | 726 736 | 8 1 820 838 | 9 0 | 9 55 1115 1148 1245 | 1 0 1 6 | .. | 1 9 | .. 135 2 0 .. 230 310 |
| Blowers Green ....| 6 1 | .. | 631 | .. | 643 | .. | .. | 7 1 | 7 8 | 713 | .. 739 | 8 4 | .. 841 | .. .. | 1151 1248 | .. 1 9 | .. 138 .. .. 233 .. |
| Baptist End Halt..| 6 3 | .. | 633 | .. | 645 | .. | .. | 7 3 | .. | 716 | .. 741 | 8 6 | .. 843 | .. .. | 1153 1250 | .. 1 11 | .. 140 .. .. 235 .. |
| Windmill End ....| 6 6 | .. | 636 | .. | 647 | .. | .. | 7 6 | 714 | 790 | .. 744 | 8 9 | .. 846 | .. .. | 1156 1253 | .. 1 14 | .. 143 .. .. 238 .. |
| Darby End Halt..| 6 8 | .. | 638 | .. | 649 | .. | .. | 7 8 | .. | 792 | .. 746 | 811 | .. 848 | .. .. | 1158 1255 | .. 1 16 | .. 145 .. .. 240 .. |
| Old Hill (H.S.) H.| 610 | .. | 640 | .. | 651 | .. | .. | 710 | .. | 725 | .. 748 | 813 | .. 850 | .. .. | 12 0 1257 | .. 1 18 | .. 147 .. .. 242 .. |
| Old Hill ¶ ....ar.| 612 | .. | 642 | .. | 653 | .. | .. | 712 | 719 | 727 | .. 750 | 815 | .. 852 | .. .. | 12 2 1259 | .. 1 20 | .. 149 .. .. 244 .. |
| Old Hill ....dp. | .. | 620 | 649 | .. | .. | 7 0 | 7 10 | .. | 721 | 736 | .. 8 1 | 821 | .. 858 | .. .. | 1221 | .. | 1 30 | .. 2 9 3 4 .. |
| Rowley R. & Bkht| .. | 626 | 654 | .. | .. | 7 57 | 7 15 | .. | 727 | 741 | .. 8 7 | .. | 9 3 | .. .. | 1225 | .. | 1 35 | .. 214 3 9 .. |
| Oldbury & L.G.dp.| .. | 631 | 659 | .. | .. | 7 97 | 20 | .. | 731 | 746 | .. 812 | .. | 9 7 | .. .. | 1229 | .. | 1 39 | .. 218 313 .. |
| Smethwick J'tion | .. | 635 | 7 4 | .. | .. | 714 | 7 24 | .. | 736 | 750 | .. 816 | 831 | .. 911 | .. .. | 1233 | .. | 1 43 | .. 222 317 .. |
| Great Bridge .. | .. | .. | .. | 7 3 | .. | .. | .. | .. | .. | 733 | .. | 827 | .. 9 7 10 2 1122 | .. .. | 1 7 | .. | 2 7 .. 316 |
| Swan Village ..dp.| .. | .. | .. | 7 6 | .. | .. | .. | .. | .. | 736 | .. | 830 | .. 9 10 10 5 1125 | .. .. | 110 | .. | 210 .. 319 |
| West Bromwich ..| .. | .. | .. | 710 | .. | .. | .. | .. | .. | 740 | .. | 834 | .. 9 13 10 9 1128 | .. .. | 114 | .. | 213 .. 322 |
| H'sw'h & Smth'k dp.| .. | 640 | 7 9 | 715 | .. | 719 | 7 29 | .. | 741 | 755 | 745 821 | 835 839 916 | 9 18 1014 1133 1238 | .. .. | 119 | .. | 1 47 | .. 226 321 327 |
| Soho & Winson Gn.| .. | 643 | .. | .. | .. | .. | 7 32 | .. | 744 | 758 | .. 824 | .. | .. 919 | .. .. | 1241 | .. | 1 50 | .. 229 324 .. |
| Hockley .........| .. | 647 | 715 | 720 | .. | 724 | 7 35 | .. | 747 | 8 1 | 750 828 | .. | .. 922 9 21 | .. 1136 1244 | .. 123 | .. | 1 53 | .. 232 327 .. |
| Birmingham S.H.ar.| .. | 651 | 721 | 726 | .. | 727 | 7 39 | .. | 752 | 8 5 | 753 832 | 841 845 925 | 9 25 1020 1140 1248 | .. 126 | .. | 1 57 | .. 223 235 331 335 |

WEEK DAYS      SUNDAYS

| | pm pm pm pm | SX | S p.m. | p.m. | SX | p.m. | p.m. p.m. p.m. | p.m p.m p.m | | a.m. a.m. p.m p.m p.m p.m |
|---|---|---|---|---|---|---|---|---|---|---|
| Dudley ........dp. | 327 .. 420 | .. | 514 5 17 525 5 56 6 | 5 | 624 645 7 4 | .. | 7 45 8 0 9 15 9 25 1025 | | 9 30 11 5 2 5 5 10 7 10 8 50 |
| Blowers Green .. | 330 .. 423 | .. | 5 20 528 5 59 | .. | 627 | .. 7 7 | .. 7 48 | .. 9 18 | .. 1028 | | .. .. .. .. .. .. .. |
| Baptist End Halt | 332 .. 425 | .. | 5 22 530 6 1 | .. | 629 | .. 7 9 | .. 7 50 | .. 9 20 | .. 1030 | | .. .. .. .. .. .. .. |
| Windmill End .. | 335 .. 428 | .. | 5 25 533 6 4 | .. | 632 | .. 7 12 | .. 7 53 | .. 9 23 | .. 1033 | | .. .. .. .. .. .. .. |
| Darby End Halt | 337 .. 430 | .. | 5 27 535 6 6 | .. | 634 | .. 7 14 | .. 7 55 | .. 9 25 | .. 1035 | | .. .. .. .. .. .. .. |
| Old Hill (H.S.) H.| 339 .. 432 | .. | 5 29 537 6 8 | .. | 636 | .. 7 16 | .. 7 57 | .. 9 27 | .. 1037 | | .. .. .. .. .. .. .. |
| Old Hill ....ar.| 341 .. 434 | .. | 5 31 539 6 10 | .. | 638 | .. 7 18 | .. 7 59 | .. 9 29 | .. 1039 | | .. .. .. .. .. .. .. |
| Old Hill ....dp. | 351 .. 443 | .. | .. .. .. | .. | 630 | .. .. | 7 51 8 35 | .. 9 35 | .. 1045 | | .. .. .. .. .. .. .. |
| Rowley R. & Bkht| 356 .. 448 | .. | .. .. .. | .. | 635 | .. .. | 7 56 8 40 | .. 9 40 | .. 1050 | | .. .. .. .. .. .. .. |
| Oldbury & L.G.dp.| 4 0 .. 452 | .. | .. .. .. | .. | 639 | .. .. | 8 1 8 44 | .. 9 44 | .. 1054 | | .. .. .. .. .. .. .. |
| Smethwick J'tion | 4 4 .. 456 | .. | .. .. .. | .. | 643 | .. .. | 8 5 8 48 | .. 9 48 | .. 1058 | | .. .. .. .. .. .. .. |
| Great Bridge | .. .. .. | 522 | .. .. 6 12 | .. | 652 | .. .. | 8 7 .. | .. 9 31 | .. .. | | 9 36 1112 2 115 16 7 17 8 57 |
| Swan Village ..dp.| .. .. .. | 525 | .. .. 6 15 | .. | 655 | .. .. | 8 10 .. | .. 9 34 | .. .. | | 9 39 1115 2 145 197 20 9 0 |
| West Bromwich ..| .. .. .. | 529 | .. .. 6 19 | .. | 658 | .. .. | 8 14 .. | .. 9 37 | .. .. | | 9 43 1119 2 185 227 23 9 3 |
| H'sw'h & Smth dp.| 4 8 .. 5 1 | 534 | .. .. 6 24 | 648 | .. 7 3 | 8 10 8 53 | 8 19 9 53 9 42 11 3 | | 9 47 1123 2 225 277 28 9 8 |
| Soho & Winson Gn.| 411 .. 5 4 | .. | .. .. .. | 651 | .. .. | 8 13 8 56 | .. 9 56 .. | | .. .. .. 5 307 319 11 |
| Hockley .........| 414 .. 5 8 | 538 | .. .. .. | 654 | .. .. | 8 16 9 0 8 22 10 0 | .. 11 8 | | .. .. .. 5 337 349 14 |
| Birmingham S.H. ar.| 417 .. 512 | 541 | .. .. 6 33 | 658 | 710 .. | 8 20 9 4 8 26 10 4 | 9 48 1112 | | 9 54 1130 2 29 5 367 379 17 |

S—Sats. only.     SX—Sats. ex.     ¶—Road Motor Service runs between Old Hill and Halesowen.

100 *A 'Jubilee' class engine with express train runs into Dudley Port station.*

The official opening of the Dudley to Cradley Heath tram took place on 19 October 1900 after trial runs beginning on 11 July, and the first service car arrived in Cradley Heath at 1.40 on 29 September. Rowley Regis UDC was keen to have a tram service from Blackheath to Old Hill but, although it is easy enough to walk down the hill via Waterfall Lane or Moor Lane in twenty minutes, the difficulty is walking back again, and trams had little chance of negotiating either steep route, where both lanes were narrow. A small estate at 'the Tump' was bought, and a new road constructed running round the steep hill in the manner of continental hairpin bends. Known as Perry Park Road, the new route was still a hard grind for the trams which shuttled backwards and forwards between Blackheath and Old Hill Cross. (Midland Red buses were still doing the same on the 232 route until the advent of the West Midlands

county.) Plans to provide a tram service from Blackheath to Oldbury came to nothing, but the trams began running up Perry Park Road on 19 November 1904. Tram services were never to be paramount in Rowley borough and the first Midland Red from Cradley Heath to Brierley Hill ran on 6 February that year.

The main route through Rowley Regis UDC was that serving Dudley, Burnt Tree, Tividale, Brades and Oldbury, and on to Smethwick and Birmingham. The route, nicknamed 'the track' by bus drivers in the 1940s and '50s because the old tram lines remained down the centre of the road for many years, has proved a constant winner. Converted to electric operation in 1904, the Birmingham and Midland Tramways Ltd route had a regular twenty-minute service which was sometimes increased to ten minutes. Numbered 87 in August 1928, the tram route survived until September 1939,

101   *The railway bridge over John's Lane at Tividale.*

102   *The mineral line embankment at Warren's Hall is now a footpath, with trees growing on the side of the old bank.*

# THOMAS WILLIAM LENCH LIMITED

P. O. BOX No 3
EXCELSIOR WORKS
**BLACKHEATH**
BIRMINGHAM

TELEPHONE · BLACKHEATH 1151 (10 LINES)

TELEGRAMS · LENCHONIA, BLACKHEATH, BIRMINGHAM

YOUR REF

OUR REF

**103**  *Letterhead of Thomas Lench, 1962.*

becoming B87 when Midland Red buses were introduced but reverting to 87 after the inauguration of the West Midland Passenger Transport Authority. Thus the same route number has guided passengers through Tividale for nearly eighty years. It is now run by buses from West Bromwich garage and is one of the first routes from that garage to be operated by kneeling double-deckers.

A site central to the tramways system (though not to Rowley Regis) was sought for a tram shed and repair works. Land formerly belonging to Brindfield or Tividale Hall was bought and developed by Birmingham and Midland Tramways at a cost of £3,193. The repair works would be used by the group of Black Country companies operating trams in the area. Tividale works put together tram components delivered from bodymakers Brush with their heavy trucks and included a tram shed for working cars. The tram shed and works remained an important element in the Black Country tram system until 1930, when the system was rapidly being replaced by buses and trolleybuses run by the various local authorities. Only Birmingham retained trams after this, continuing to run the 87 route from West Smethwick depot until just after the outbreak of the Second World War.

In February 1908 a spectacular accident involving a Birmingham and Midland Tramway Company car made the national newspapers. At Gypsy Lane (City Road) tram overturned, pinning down the conductor, who was killed. The driver jumped out of his cab, but all 16 passengers were hurt in some way, three of them being detained in hospital. There was evidence given at the Board of Trade enquiry that the tram had been recently overhauled at Tividale works. The driver said he had observed the 4 m.p.h. speed limit in the passing loop by Gypsy Lane, and had accelerated as soon as he left the loop. The chairman, suspecting that a broken wheel had caused the problem, interrogated Mr R.F. Brown of Harborne, a company engineer, very particularly about the wheel system used.

The actual track along this route was always dubious and trams would sway and pitch despite the 12 m.p.h. limit. An expert witness examined it for the enquiry and found a discrepancy of well over an inch and a half in the height of the two rails. This may have caused the front wheel of the tram to jump the track at the exit from the loop, with disastrous consequences, although Colonel Yorke, for the Board of Trade, said in his report that the inequality of the track did not cause the accident. He thought the cause was the left-hand trailing wheel. *The Electric Review* considered the design and manufacture of the wheel had been a major cause and commended the company for replacing the design with a more conventional one. It is still impossible to tell what caused the Gypsy Lane derailment, but suspicions about the very rocky track must remain.

A superb fictional picture of the Cradley Heath to Dudley tram ride is given in Halesowen author Francis Brett Young's *Black Diamond* (1921). John Fellows is going to the fair in Dudley with his family on August Bank Holiday. They wait for twenty minutes for 'one of those reckless tramway-cars that go roaring like spent shells through all the wastes of the black country'. The tram arrives and they board, but

They could not speak for the jolt and jangle of its progress, for the clanging of its bell and the alarming sputter of electric sparks when it swayed on its springs and threatened to jump the rails. In their four miles of journey they could see no green. They passed through endless streets of grimy brick … Even though the fires of the furnaces and factories had been banked down for the holidays they could still smell the heat which had scorched and blackened this volcanic country on every side.

Such, in Brett Young's eyes, was the journey from Cradley Heath via Old Hill and Netherton to the playground of Dudley Castle woods. The route finally closed on 31 December 1929.

**104** *The last remains of Grovelands Farm.*

**105** *Shakespeare's works in Cox's Lane, Old Hill, with Netherton in the background.*

106 *An impression
of Doulton's Pottery.*

A frequent sight in parts of Rowley Regis from the 19th century until well into the 20th was the network of narrow gauge mineral railways transporting coal, ironstone and other minerals from mines and quarries to the works for processing or to the canals for onward transport. Many of these worked on the 'incline' principle. Trucks, often coupled together into trains, ran (sometimes on rather shaky lines) down a slope to their destination. They were generally cable-operated, though when there was no useful incline horses or, alternatively, steam engines hauled some of the tubs. Short tunnels and bridges had to be constructed to carry the ropeways over or under roads. Perhaps the most prominent was the 'Revo' bridge (so called because of its brightly painted advertisement) over the Birmingham New Road. This incline ran from Darby's Hill to a canal basin at Tividale, while a second line ran down from Grace Mary colliery to Brades Hall locks.

Relics of these mineral lines are few and far between, but at Warren's Hall the embankment still exists, now covered with trees, while near Cobbs Engine House, a little lower down the country park, the mineral line bridge still spans the canal, providing a fine view of the south entrance to the Netherton Tunnel. Two other mineral lines nearby lead from Springfield and from Hailstone quarry to the canal basin opposite Doulton's works. Both once ran beneath the Dudley Road, but it is not easy now to see the exact location. A mineral line embankment can still be seen near Haden Hill Park.

Tramways once transported coal to Corngreaves iron works, some of which were engine-hauled. A particularly splendid line ran along the back of St Luke's churchyard, past the end of Plant Street and on an embankment across Halesowen Road in front of Holy Trinity, then across Wright's Lane and the Great Western Railway to the canal basins near the Fly colliery. Near Rowley Village

**107** *Blackheath Market, with the spire of the Birmingham Road church, former home of Birmingham Road Methodists (Sandwell Archives ephemera).*

**108** *Blackheath High Street about 1915.*

**109**   *Children at the Endowed Day School, c.1885.*

the Bell End line formed a loop round the colliery and ran across what had once been Rowley demesne, then across Throne Road to reach the Titford Canal at a basin over the boundary in Oldbury. Sixty or more years ago these mineral lines were a prominent feature of the landscape, and it is unfortunate that so little remains of them.

Rowley Regis borough was often thought of as not much more than a sandwich between larger areas, and it was the interests of Birmingham, Dudley and Wolverhampton which caused a major transport change in the first half of the 20th century. This was the design and building of the 'New Road', alternatively called the Wolverhampton Road

**110**   *Looking up Waterfall Lane in 1960.*

or the Birmingham New Road according to which part of the area one lived in. Old routes from Wolverhampton to Birmingham were slow and congested, and a fine new route was decided on by the leadership of Birmingham City Council. At its south-east end, Wolverhampton Road South cut between Harborne and Quinton and went on to Northfield. It entered Rowley just after passing Bury Hill Park, and after crossing City Road and going beneath the Revo bridge left the borough for Dudley near to Hill Road. This became the arterial route from Dudley to Birmingham, and now to the motorway junction at Birchley, and is served by the 126 bus (originally the 125). The road was opened by the Prince of Wales on 2 November 1927 and for a short while provided the opportunity for newly bought cars to reach 100 m.p.h. Nowadays, a strict 40 m.p.h. limit is enforced by frequent speed cameras.

Bus services in Rowley during the mid-20th century were dominated by the Midland Red, with its garage at Cradley Heath running service single and double-deckers, and also housing some long-distance coaches. Arterial routes included the 243 and 244 to Dudley, replacing the Cradley Heath tram, and the Birmingham to Dudley No.140 service via Blackheath. Midland Red was nationalised, then West Midland Transport regionalised, under the Passenger Transport Authority, and

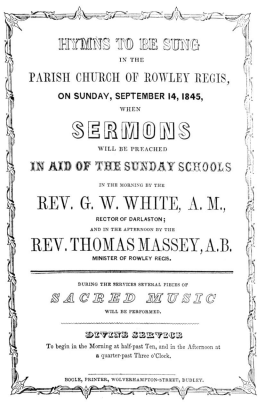

111 *Notice of service at Rowley church, 1845.*

then privatised so that many services passed into the hands of National Bus. Cradley Heath garage was closed and the site sold; many different garages have since run services to Cradley Heath. At the time of writing they include West Bromwich, Pensnett and Liverpool Street in Birmingham.

# XI

# Rowley Parish Church and the Church of England

At the start of the 19th century George Barrs had quickly come to the conclusion that the church building could not be repaired and strove to persuade parishioners that total replacement was the only solution. In the 1920s the Rev. F.C. Cheverton was in the same position. Faced with the enormous task of rebuilding Rowley church, he determined to emphasise the unusual fact of 'four churches on this site'. This idea took strong hold and has obscured the continuity and historical value of the building on the summit of the hill which formed Rowley Village, but even now elements of the pre-Barrs church remain.

What George Barrs did for the historical record, however, was to write copiously about his Rowley Regis experiences. From his account of them and from other contemporary material we can begin to build up an accurate picture of the medieval church, disastrously mauled as it had been. We need to treat Barrs' description carefully, bearing in mind that he was no architect and was writing before Rickman's classification of medieval architecture became well known. Consequently, the church was 'Saxo-Gothic'. Its walls were partly of Rowley stone and three-quarters of a yard in thickness (although much of the walling was filled with rubble). The inside had been much plastered, but was still extremely damp.

There were two aisles, one towards the north and a much narrower one towards the south. Between these we may picture box pews that we know had been erected piecemeal as a result of various 'faculties' like the one taken out by James Raybould on 31 October 1776 in 'the middle isle' which measured 6ft by 3ft 7in. In 1777 the church was already in a decayed state, with walls propped and cramped. A 'church brief' had been issued, allowing collections to be made in other churches to repair Rowley church, but this appears to have had no success. Unfortunately few other faculties have survived. One was granted in 1699 to the Hadens and others for a gallery 18 feet long. A 'singing loft' was built in 1747 in the north part of the chancel.

The north and east walls of the chancel had been rebuilt in brick, as had the porch, which emphasises the unworkable nature of Rowley stone. The east part of the south wall was of Rowley rag, with buttresses. The upper part of this wall from the height of 12 feet was of red-grey sandstone, with a castellation on top. 'Massive octagon pillars' divided the chancel from the nave; Barrs does not say how many, but we might guess at two. The south gallery was supported by medieval pillars chopped off at the top, which had perhaps been topped by arches to hold up the roof. The windows once had 'workmanship of no ordinary character' but only one retained its original form, the rest having been enlarged to let light into the church. Under the pews was bare earth, and Barrs records having to walk through mud and water to the reading desk.

The western end of the south wall had had its parapet removed and a new roof put over it, perhaps in 1617, with dormer windows added to let light into the gallery. The roof in Barrs' day was covered with red tiles. He is very disparaging about the whole, which he says 'now extremely resembles a barn or warehouse rather than a place of worship'. The only monument mentioned is the wood-carved record of the 1617 re-roofing, on the north wall, with the names of John Russell and Humphrey Bartley, churchwardens, and

the Caddicks of Dudley, carpenters, but we know that there were more, including charity boards on the west wall near the tower. It is likely that the west door was rarely if ever opened. Whether any of Lady Monins' hatchments survived is unknown. We know that the Haden tomb was in the body of the church because, in 1686, 'Mr Haden' paid 3s. 4d. for 'breaking he church floor' [to bury a relative].

Details of the charity boards were recorded for the Charity Commissioners' enquiry in 1823. Table 1 concerned Lady Monins' deed of 1703 of £10 a year for poor children to be taught to read and write, John Moore's gift of £50 for the poor to be distributed on St Thomas' Day, William Turton of West Bromwich's gift of 13s. 4d.

## ST LUKE'S CHURCHYARD 1960s

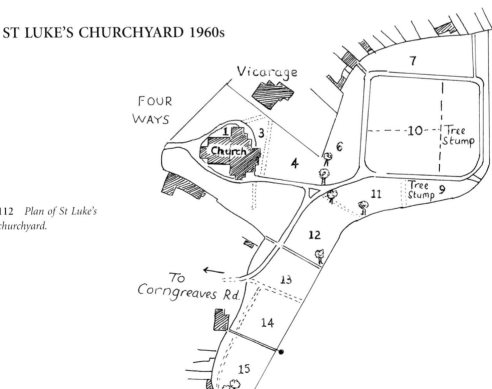

112   *Plan of St Luke's churchyard.*

a year for the poor, and John Turton [of Rowley Hall], who gave £10 capital by his will in 1714, the interest to be used for the poor. Thomas Newby's gift of a two-acre plot in Warley Wigorn was also recorded on this table. Table 2 detailed the setting up of the Mackmillan Educational Trust, which will be dealt with later. Table 3 listed recent gifts by Thomas Aynsworth, 'nail ironmonger', Mrs Phoebe Parkes, Mr Chellingworth, maltster, the Rev. Stephenson (also connected with the charity school at Reddal Hill – the commissioners added that Thomas Sidaway of Reddall Hill House had given £46 for the same purpose). Table 4, like Table 1, dealt with earlier gifts: those of Eliza White (£5); Mary Payton, £30 (this was attested by Richard Bate and Benjamin Sidaway, churchwardens for 1760); John Turton of the Brades presented the Old Hill almshouses to the poor of Rowley in 1688 (these almshouses were located off High Street, between what became Queen Street and The Cross); John Thurling gifted £10 in 1703, Alice Chambers £10 in 1615, John Sparry of Clent £10, and William Russell 'of this parish' £5. This was attested by James Mackmillan and Samuel Smart, churchwardens in 1749.

George Barrs was slightly more enamoured of the church tower. Its appearance about 1832 can be seen in the illustration on page ten. It would seem that the building had originally been of Rowley rag, but the worn corners had been replaced at some point by another stone which had been used for the upper stage of the tower including the bell tower windows. Unless his description is misleading, this must have been done in the medieval period. The detail of the work above the windows and the gargoyles at the angles of the highest stage sounds like 14th- or 15th-century work. When the new church was built this tower was retained.

The solution to Barrs' financial problems came when it was decided to sell off glebe land at Blackheath allotted under the Enclosure Act. On 6 July 1838 plans made by the architect Mr Bourne were ready to be studied by the Vestry and a temporary building was put up in a field nearby. This was destroyed by a hurricane and it was suggested that the bricks be used to make a new churchyard wall. Meanwhile work was done on buttressing and perhaps underpinning the tower, but bad weather hampered the rebuilding and work resumed in February 1841 after a hard frost. Death overtook George Barrs so that he never saw the completion of his life-long project, but the new church was opened on 8 September 1841.

From 1846 William Crump was curate of Rowley, but in 1855 a parish was finally created under an Act of 21 June 1841 and he became vicar. It is unclear when the tower of the old church was replaced, but Crump seems to imply that it remained until 1858, the year after he wrote a poetic tribute. Later illustrations show a highly ornate Gothic tower, but it did not last long for the church was declared unsafe due to mining operations and closed in 1894. The tower was shortened, but is seen in photographs taken during the first years of the new century. The body of the church was taken down and the base of the south wall remains as a memorial. The next building was begun in 1904 and, despite the later fire, some of this remains, including the foundation stone. Building began at the east end and was complete by 1907. In 1905 Rowley, including Blackheath but not Old Hill or Cradley Heath, became part of the new Birmingham diocese.

The most spectacular event in Rowley for many years occurred on 18 June 1913, when the recently completed new church was set alight. Firemen arrived to find no water supply, and

113   *St Luke's church, Cradley Heath, from the south.*

114   *Knowle Methodist church, photographed in 2005.*

115  *Rowley parish church as rebuilt by George Barrs.*

had to cut off water to Quinton and Warley before they could get enough pressure. The new pitch pine woodwork burned fiercely and the whole church was soon a raging inferno. Some firemen turned their attention to saving the parish chest, containing 400 years of records. They attached four ropes to it but these soon burned through. It was very fortunate that the old registers had mostly been copied by Miss Auden and printed by Staffordshire Parish Register Society. One of them was still with her when the fire occurred. The firemen worked hard to put out the flames, but when the chest was opened the registers were in poor condition and many other documents charred. Most of the registers were unreadable by the 1960s, and one had been completely destroyed, so without Miss Auden's work there would have remained only tantalisingly unreadable

evidence for Rowley's past. As it is, we do not have a list of the documents which were wholly burnt and discarded.

This event seemed to underline the ill luck of the old parish church. Scapegoats were sought and the *County Express* declared that the incident was an 'outrage'. Mysterious women had been seen in Old Hill, who were thought to be suffragettes, but this rumour has been discounted. The church was still in the process of being insured – five days later it would have been so – and the fire was an enormous blow to the parish. The font was cracked in pieces, and some brass Haden memorials dating from 1717 were seriously damaged. Soon after this war broke out, and there was little to be done by way of restoration until it was over.

A new vicar was appointed in 1920, the Rev. F.C. Cheverton, a retired army officer.

He set about raising the money to rebuild the church in the positive frame of mind induced by a war won, laying stress on the idea that four churches had been built on the site, although in fact much of the 1904 church was saved. The tower, retained from the 1840 building and possibly containing some part of the earlier tower, had to go, though the bells had strangely survived. A smaller tower, more in keeping with the new brick building, was designed. The parish magazine for the next few years is full of Cheverton's efforts to acquire the money needed for the new project. He fostered links with the new diocese in order to support his aims and bit by bit the money came in, an enthusiastic congregation refusing to be beaten. Cheverton was also assiduous in preserving other pieces of local history, making a plea for the retention of the village pound and depositing documents in Birmingham archives. In 1931, however, he took a second retirement, moving to Byfleet in Surrey.

By the mid-19th century it was clear that Rowley parish was much too big, Cradley Heath, Old Hill, Tividale and Blackheath having mushroomed into existence. Though many nonconformist places of worship had sprung up, Church of England effort had been concentrated on rebuilding the parish church. Cradley Heath was the first area to receive its own place of worship, when St Luke's (called 'Reddall Hill') was consecrated in February 1847. Originally it had twin turrets on the front facing Four Ways, but in 1928 these were removed during restoration work. Since many chapels had no graveyard St Luke's was at one time a repository of the respectable dead of Cradley Heath, whatever their denomination, and there were many large, even ostentatious, tombstones. An early burial is that of John Plant, who died 10 August 1853 aged 65; he was joined by his wife Mary, who died ten years later. He gave his name to Plant Street. The first vicar, Frederick James Clarke, is among slightly later interments. He had married Eliza Nock of Broadhidley in Northfield, and his father-in-law and two sons were buried in the same grave.

116  *Rowley parish church after 1904.*

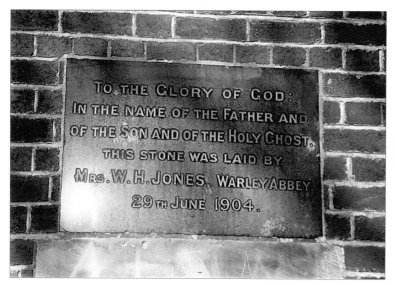

117   *The foundation stone of the 'third' church, in the rear wall of the present church.*

Blackheath had grown on both sides of the parish boundary. It was decided to remove the Rowley part of the parish, add to it parts of Halesowen and Quinton, and create the new parish of St Paul's, with the church built some way beyond Rowley's boundary. The foundation stone was laid on 18 April 1868 and the registers date from 1869. Meanwhile, the Bassano family, who had inherited some of the mining interests of the Haden family and now lived in a new house at Haden Cross, proved great benefactors to Old Hill. They gave generously to the building of a new parish church, Holy Trinity, in 1876, for which a parish had been carved from Rowley and Reddal Hill two years earlier. The impressive Trinity school rooms were added later in the 19th century, on old Haden land fronting what was by this time called Halesowen Road. In 1874 work began on a large red brick church at Tividale, just on the edge of Rowley parish, for which a new parish was created in 1878 by taking in a part of Tipton. St Michael's was the only Anglo-Catholic church in the old borough and famous for its colourful street processions. It became far too big for the neighbourhood towards the end of the 20th century, however, and was demolished in 1980.

# XII

# Nonconformist Churches and Chapels

The churchwarden's response to the 1676 Compton return suggested, if we read it correctly, that 384 parishioners failed to attend the parish church regularly. One reason must have been the inaccessible nature of the church and the inhospitable nature of the leaky building, but it might also be the low church attitude and politics of some of the leading gentry. We have already mentioned the case of William Turton, linked as he was to the family from Grovelands and the Brades. Henry Haden's attitude 'reading pamphlets' in the service when church-warden suggests that Rowley people were unenthusiastic about high-church doctrine. The house of George Colborne was licensed for nonconformist worship on 22 July 1672 and John Turton's on 5 September 1672. Nonconformity also flourished in nearby Netherton and Cradley.

Registrations of nonconformist chapels do not always state precisely where the chapel is, or indeed the exact denomination. It is, therefore, sometimes a little difficult to identify particular chapels with specific registrations. For example, an early

118  *Providence Strict Baptist Chapel, Mincing Lane.*

**119** *Christ Church, Cradley Heath, with Five Ways in the distance.*

registration of 1774 is at 'Tyler's Green', which does not exist. But when we read that Samuel Lowe and George Mackmillan were the proponents, we can guess that 'Tyler's' means Stilehouse, which may have been an Independent chapel, possibly with no descendants. In 1791 there is recorded an 'edifice or building lately erected at Bildock's Green, Rowley Regis, registered for Protestant dissenters by James Sidaway and others'. There is no such place as Bildock's Green, but an open patch at Cradley Heath was called Piddock's Green, and the name of Sidaway, associated with Reddall Hill House, confirms this guess.

During the first forty years of the 19th century there were many new registrations, leading to the proliferation of chapels which is still evident throughout the former borough of Rowley Regis. Two principal streams of nonconformity can be discerned: Baptists and Methodists. Each of these divided into two

again: Primitive Methodism, with its Calvinist element, and Wesleyan, more Universalist; and a similar divide among Baptists between 'General' Baptists and the 'Strict & Particular' group. All are still represented in Rowley. There are also chapels which do not belong to either of these strands, such as the 'Garden Church' at Siviter's Lane.

It is not surprising that early nonconformism developed at Tividale, which was cut off from the main centre of Rowley at Rowley Village. Here, in December 1812, a house occupied by Richard Jeffries was registered as a place of worship for dissenters. Timothy and Thomas Tilley stood as witnesses, with John Sturges and John Hornblower. It is not clear which chapel this refers to, though, as early directories have more to say about taverns and public houses than chapels. A plan of 1829 shows two small rows of cottages on the opposite side of Dudley Road from Tividale Hall, but there are few other buildings.

John Wesley is said to have visited Rowley parish. He was in nearby Quinton in 1781 and again, at the house of Ambrose Foley, in 1785. A rhyme about his visit to Rowley circulates in the area:

> John Wesley had a bonny horse,
> the bonniest e'er yo'n sin;
> They took 'im down to Haysich brook
> and shoved him yedfust in.

I have been surprised to find that this is a version of a similar rhyme found in other parts of the country, but it might be worth noting that Hayseech Methodist Chapel is of Primitive origin, not Wesleyan. In fact, it is possible that Primitive Methodism is the dominant form in Rowley Regis, though such distinctions have now largely disappeared.

A case in point is the once formidable Grainger's Lane Chapel. This appears to have begun with preaching by James Bonser in 1820, which led to a nucleus of Primitive Methodists being formed in Cradley Heath by 1821. They began by using a nailers' shop in Tibbetts' Gardens (variously spelt), which was probably erected after the Enclosure Award. By 1827 there were 36 members, including six members of the Billingham family and six of the Tibbetts. The prime mover, William Tibbetts, was buried at St Luke's after his death on 8 November 1855.

The first chapel at Grainger's Lane was erected shortly before 1829, perhaps converted from two cottages, and was registered on 12 June 1829. A new church followed in 1841, surmounted by a splendid clock, which became known as the clock chapel. The clock had been sponsored by Mr John Tibbetts, who left £100 for the purpose. Writing in 1910, Samuel Woodhouse described the scene in Cradley Heath about 1845, when Cradley Road was called just 'the common'. Land here was set out in small allotments and known as the 'Beacher Ground'. From there

**120** *Tividale (Tipton Road) Methodist Church in 2005.*

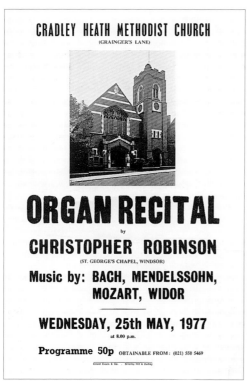

CRADLEY HEATH METHODIST CHURCH
(GRAINGER'S LANE)

# ORGAN RECITAL
by
## CHRISTOPHER ROBINSON
(ST. GEORGE'S CHAPEL, WINDSOR)
### Music by: BACH, MENDELSSOHN, MOZART, WIDOR

**WEDNESDAY, 25th MAY, 1977**
at 8.00 p.m.

**Programme 50p** OBTAINABLE FROM : (021) 550 5469

**121**   *Advertisement for an organ recital at Grainger's Lane Methodist Church, Cradley Heath, in 1977.*

to Lodge Forge was the Grainger Estate, with the stately hall in the centre. This was 'of county style, square, three storeys in height, with bow windows back and front, and usual sash windows above'. Kitchen gardens and orchards surrounded it. There were two small ponds in front of the house, and a path led through the fields to Cradley. The hall was demolished when the Great Western Railway built the Stourbridge to Birmingham line in 1865, and the land was sold off for building, much of it given over to the Stour colliery.

Grainger's Lane Primitive Methodist Chapel was enlarged in 1858, but in 1895 there was considerable mining subsidence, and the old clock chapel had to be deserted. A new church was built nine years later, which had the advantage of new school rooms, brick-

built in a style part Norman and part Early English. They were typical of much Sunday school building of the day and, though by no means as large, echoed the style of Trinity school rooms at Old Hill, without the stone dressing. Prominent among the families attending and supporting the church were the Woodhouses, chainmakers and general benefactors.

An early proponent of nonconformity in Rowley Village was Joseph Parkes, who registered a room in his house in January 1821 for 'Protestant Dissenters'. He is possibly father or grandfather of Joseph Parkes of Hackett Street, who wrote the hymn tune 'Rowley Regis' and other tunes once well known in the area. The original Wesleyan Methodist church at Old Hill was registered in June 1829 and built by 1830. Its successor in Halesowen Road still remains but is not in use.

The registration of 'a building' for General Baptists at Four Ways, Cradley Heath, was recorded in January 1847, the minister being Thomas Bannister. The trustees were Benjamin Fellows and John Billingham. A General Baptist chapel at Rowley Village was licensed in 1823, the prime movers being John and James Adams, but the initiative soon seems to have passed to the Strict Baptists. Spurred on by George Barrs' evangelical preaching, but disagreeing with his views on infant baptism, Daniel Matthews preached at the Baptist Chapel, which he soon attached to the Strict Baptist cause. In 1829 he took over a small warehouse belonging to Thomas Sidaway at Reddal Hill, which appears to be the origin of Spring Meadow Chapel. There is a little confusion in the documentation, but it seems that it was this building which was constituted a Strict Baptist chapel in 1833, which removed to its present site in 1841. Unlike the other nonconformist groups,

Strict Baptists had their own graveyards and Spring Meadow graveyard was enlarged in 1876. At this time the Baptists, who had rejected the installation of church organs, had an orchestra consisting of five violins, cello, bass, cornet and serpent, a large wind instrument. Hymns sung at the chapel have generally been based on those of Isaac Watts. A daughter chapel, Ebenezer, was founded at Station Road, Old Hill in 1903.

Two other Strict Baptist chapels must be mentioned, Cave Adullam and Providence. During the life of George Barrs, one of his followers had been Joseph Bowater of Gorsty Hill; he was not satisfied with the preaching of Barrs' successors, and decided to build a small chapel near his house. In course of time this became too small, and in about 1884 it was decided to move to a new site in what was then called Tump Road (Beeches Road, Blackheath). The new chapel was opened on Easter Tuesday 1898. The splendid building at Bell End, Providence Chapel, derives from the chapel in Rowley Village founded by Daniel Matthews. Negotiations for it began in 1876 and the present building began to be erected soon after. Twenty years later a group of members led by Joseph Ruston, unhappy at the introduction of an organ, seceded and built Ebenezer Chapel on Hawes Lane.

Close to the Wesleyan theology was the Methodist 'New Connexion', represented in Old Hill by Zion's Hill Church, nearly opposite Holy Trinity. The building still exists at the time of writing, though its use has changed several times. Many other Methodist churches were built in the borough, though some have now been amalgamated and, in some cases, built new churches. The most spectacular of all, perhaps, is Birmingham Road, Blackheath. With its spire, this red-brick building looks more like an Anglican church and is a prominent feature of the

Blackheath landscape. Though no longer Methodist, it seems likely to maintain a Christian presence in this part of Blackheath. The chief Wesleyan church in Rowley itself was Hawes Lane, built in 1862 near the Club Buildings. Further along the road to Dudley, Knowle Methodist church was erected in 1868. A presence still remains in buildings which have been much modified.

Not all the chapels in Rowley can be covered here, but no local person will forget the 'rhubarb' chapel which used to stand at Old Hill Cross. In a dominant position opposite the main road to Cradley Heath, the church was actually called St James'. It was opened in 1876 but was hardly ever known by its real name. No one is quite sure why it was nicknamed the 'rhubarb' chapel, but one suggestion is that it was built on fields

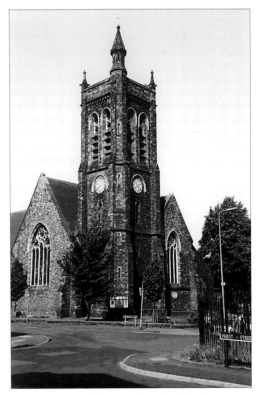

122  *Holy Trinity church, Old Hill.*

**123**  *Aerial view of Tividale in 1946. The road running across the top right of the picture is Dudley Road. The tram works can be seen above it to the right, and Tividale park at the top right.*

formerly used for growing rhubarb. Important in High Street (Highgate Street) was the Tabernacle Methodist Church, founded in 1869 with schools added in 1897. At Five Ways, Cradley Heath, an important landmark is Christ Church, a splendid red-brick building which has served several purposes since its closure as a chapel.

Black Country chapels and churches have had a profound effect on the culture of the neighbourhood and nowhere has this been more evident than in Rowley Regis. Until the mid-1980s Sunday school attendance was common, even for those whose acquaintance with churches would otherwise have been small. A vivid feature of the district were the Sunday school anniversary processions, banners held high, marching through the streets of Old Hill or Blackheath. The large

number of chapel Sunday schools meant there was room for anyone who wished to go. Lusty hymn singing was encouraged in schools, and gave rise to a respect for music in general. The playing of instruments as part of the church service, instead of merely listening to an organ, lasted until the turn of the 20th century, and a tradition was born which issued in many amateur performances of *Messiah* and other oratorios, including the popular Stainer's *Crucifixion*. Operatic societies developed here, a major example being the Tabernacle in High Street, Old Hill. Music provided by Cradley Heath Salvation Army, whose headquarters were at Newtown Lane, has often featured in performances in Birmingham city centre. Other small organisations include Darby's Hill Mission near Lye Cross, Turner's Hill.

# XIII

# Education

Lady Monins' attempt to provide for education in Rowley did not have lasting results, and by the end of the 18th century a further attempt was made to supply the need. Two Birmingham brothers, George and John Mackmillan, who then lived at Stilehouse (now the *Britannia Inn*), were instrumental in this enterprise, securing a plot of land at Reddal Hill from Lord Dudley and, with the Rev. Christopher Stephenson, establishing the first real school in Rowley in March 1790. This was followed in 1792 by the gift of land almost facing Stilehouse. A trust was set up to administer the schools and a house for the schoolmaster built in

Rowley Village in 1818. Although the Reddal Hill school developed into an LEA-run establishment, the Rowley school did not. Instead, a National School was built at Hawes Lane.

Industry required some degree of education for its operatives, and so the New British Iron Company decided to build a school in Cradley Heath on land later known as Plant Street which was opened in 1849. The building, though modified, still stands; it became the kernel of the Corngreaves complex, to which in 1887 was added a boys' school at Meredith Street, finally demolished in 1988. In time the Corngreaves foundation came

124 *Reddal Hill school in the 19th century, based on drawings and plan.*

125  *Rowley Village Endowed School, formerly opposite the* Britannia *public house.*

under the aegis of the School Board and its successors. It is a feature of education in Rowley Regis that no institution lasts long before reorganisation.

Much basic education during the 19th century was carried out by churches and chapels in Sunday schools such as the Tabernacle School in High Street, Old Hill. However, the 1870 Education Act established a framework for organised public education. Rowley Regis School Board was founded in 1874 and set about building new schools, including the Board School, Old Hill Junior, and the former Tividale Primary School, now demolished. The Blackheath School complex, for boys, girls and infants, in Powke Lane was opened on 27 October 1879 to serve the town which had blossomed in the previous two decades. Macefield School, which was later a secondary school, then merged with Heathfield and is currently the successor to Reddal Hill Primary School, also opened. Further schools were built at Plant Street, Lomey Town and at The Knowle in 1877, the last area by then beginning to be better known as Springfield.

Wrights Lane schools (Temple Meadow) exhibit a date of 1898, but the complex, known

as the Higher Grade School, was opened on 19 February 1900, the last important project of Rowley Regis School Board and the forerunner, at a considerable distance, of Rowley Regis Grammar School. A disaster was to overtake the area two years later with the passing of the 1902 Education Act, which abolished school boards, placing education in the hands of local authorities, but excluded secondary education from the urban districts. This allowed Rowley to build the Siviter's Lane complex, opened on 1 July 1904, but meant that the brave effort at Wrights Lane had to close, and much local power was transferred to Dudley. As a borough, Dudley could legally maintain grammar schools and, as part of Worcestershire, Halesowen could continue its secondary provision. Among practical consequences at Wrights Lane, French was discontinued as a teaching subject, and in 1925 the school became known as the Central School. The comparative weakness of Rowley UDC, behind which is the geographical nature of the region, has continued to influence education in the area today.

In the 1920s the Rev. F.C. Cheverton made great efforts to reunite Rowley church with the Mackmillan endowment, linking it with Hawes Lane School, which was thought of as the church school. He was unsuccessful and indeed there seems to have been a clash of interest with the trustees of the Endowed School. This school eventually became a Sunday school only, in accommodation rented from the UDC. In 1929 the Haddow Report necessitated further reorganisation, and in 1933 the raising of the UDC to borough status would cause further upset. It is impossible to detail all the changes that took place, but in the Blackheath and Rowley areas Siviter's Lane began a reputable career as a girls' school, while there were transfers from Hawes Lane to The Knowle and Powke Lane, Hawes Lane becoming Rowley Regis Hawes Lane Council Mixed Junior School on 1 October 1929, and Powke Lane becoming Blackheath Junior Mixed School.

Secondary education was now in the hands of Staffordshire Education Committee, which ran schools for the over-11s throughout the county. Rowley was part of South-west Staffs along with neighbouring Tipton and Brierley Hill. None of these areas had a grammar school, but a few children gained places at one of the Dudley schools or at Halesowen, and a small number of schools were able to find places for their pupils at King Edward's, Birmingham. But, before the lack of a grammar school could be remedied, the Second World War broke out.

There are many records and memories of school life during the late 19th and early 20th centuries. Fevers and illnesses raged and were cured by disinfecting school premises with carbolic soap and powder. Children were often away ill, but they were not allowed time off to go to Rowley Wake (about the third week in September). Sometimes teachers were sent out in the dinner hour to bring in the absentees, for attendance was almost

**126**  *First page of the log book of Wright's Lane school.*

In August there were more than 6800 outstanding cases of minor repairs waiting to be done. At the rate at which they are being dealt with it will take nearly four years to clear them.

Councillor J. Adams says that the arrears can never be cleared. We say that if there is a will, there is a way.

There has been no progress with the Blackheath Shopping Centre Development Scheme. In fact in the whole six months it has not been considered or discussed.

We shall continue our keen interest in Council affairs, particularly those affecting the Ward and this end of the Borough.

And though we are sorry that we cannot present a better picture to you, we thought you might like to have this interim report which keeps you informed of what is going on.

Yours sincerely,

J. W. SHAKESPEARE
Westfield,
Hayseech,
OLD HILL.

J. SHAKESPEARE
85 Lawrence Lane,
OLD HILL.

**127**  *Part of a leaflet from the Shakespeares, Independent councillors in Old Hill, protesting about the new Warley Council, 1966.*

128  *The rear of the hall and the library in the old grammar school.*

129  *The newly built grammar school, built by Staffordshire Council on lines similar to Brierley Hill and Tipton Grammar Schools.*

as important as learning and could be quantified for praise or blame. In 1894 physical exercises were introduced: as the head wrote in the log-book at Powke Lane, 'Recreation is now compulsory for about two hours per week'. As far back as 1881 Powke Lane boys were allowed to go at 3.45 to watch a cricket match between the school and 'Rowley National School' (Hawes Lane). Apart from illness, absences occurred because of wild beast shows and miners' strikes. Punishments were fairer and less savage than is sometimes thought, and several times the girls' school head at Powke Lane reprimands a teacher for beating a child.

Reddal Hill school, the first purpose-built school in the parish, was outgrowing its premises by the late 1870s and the old buildings were demolished in 1876. Miss Haden of the Haden Hill family provided financial support for the rebuilding, and at this time the Mackmillan Trust was still much concerned with religious and educational work. The 1902 Education Act began to loosen the link between religion and education, and as a result the Mackmillan Educational Trust, in a deed of 1903, modified the religious training clause in its original deeds. Reddal Hill was able to adjust to secular authority but, much later, the new school was demolished and the

130    *The hall of the new school.*

131    *Former Macefields School, now Reddal Hill Primary.*

**132** *Mr G.T. Lloyd, headmaster of Rowley Regis Grammar School.*

pupils were relocated to the old Macefield building.

Tividale was, as always, rather separated from the rest of the borough. Pupils from Tividale attending the school at Wrights Lane had to go to Dudley to catch a train to Old Hill. During strikes this was impossible, and school time was lost. After the Second World War Tividale became the first part of the borough for which a purpose-built comprehensive school was provided. Excellent primary schools were built at Oakham and Tividale Hall, to supplement the work of the original Tividale Primary School.

The 1944 Education Act required LEAs to provide adequate secondary schools, now divided into grammar, technical and modern. Staffordshire responded with three new grammar schools at Tipton, Brierley Hill and Rowley, pupils crossing borough boundaries but remaining in South-west Staffs. Wrights

**133** *Corngreaves Primary School. The earlier school built by Corngreaves Iron Co. is the further building.*

134 *Temple Meadow Primary School, Wright's Lane.*

135 *Borough of Rowley Regis coat of arms.*

Lane was chosen to be made up to grammar-school status and opened on 12 September 1946. For a year the head of the Central School remained in post before G.T. Lloyd was appointed as, effectively, the first head of Rowley Regis Grammar School; no better appointment could have been made.

George Lloyd was a native of the district, lived at Cradley Heath and was deeply involved in the life of the area. He had ecumenical ideas, being at home both in St Luke's and Grainger's Lane churches. In his reminiscences he writes of the outstanding weakness of the South-west Staffs division – 'one of the largest in the country' – in having no grammar school up to this point. He was determined to remedy the situation for Rowley, and carried his visionary intentions into practice. He records the comment of the Minister of Education when told that the school

136   *The cast of 'Noye's Fludde' at the grammar school.*

buildings were inadequate: 'You can do a lot with a pot of paint and imagination.' And despite efforts on the part of George Lloyd, it was fifteen years before a new building finally materialised at the top of the hill in Hawes Lane, near to where the original Hawes Lane National School had been built. The buildings in Wrights Lane were taken over by Temple Meadow Primary School. One is reminded of the drive and determination of another George, George Barrs, and the cyclical nature of things in Rowley: after forty years, Barrs got his new church, which fell down; after fifteen years, George Lloyd got his new school, which was reorganised into a sixth-form college, failed in terms of financial viability, was sold, and at the time of writing lies empty. The wheel awaits reinventing.

Shortly after the foundation of the grammar school, it became county and national policy to introduce comprehensive education. The Tividale area was self-contained, and was designated for a new school, a large green area in City Road being set aside. The Tividale area had a balanced community provided the catchment area was carefully drawn, and this was done, thus preventing children from the greater Tividale area from entering the 11-plus exam. The new school is now Tividale Secondary School and Community College. Further plans were in the pipeline, but before they could be put into operation there were to be two reorganisations of local government by which Rowley Regis was removed from Staffordshire into Worcestershire, and then into West Midlands county, although the latter never became an education authority.

# XIV

# Sports, Pastimes and Popular Culture

On 29 April 1806 four-year-old Elizabeth Round was killed, according to George Barrs, when her mother 'just stepped out of the house to part some cocks which were fighting', the little girl's clothes caught fire, and she was so badly burnt that she eventually died. In fact, inciting and training cocks to fight was the more usual attitude. Barrs waged war against cock-fighting and bull-baiting, and in the end these sports were banned. However, keeping and training animals and birds remained a Rowley Regis preoccupation, and as the 19th century turned into the 20th, this developed into the sports of whippet and greyhound racing, and keeping and racing pigeons. Other sports and entertainments, such as football, cricket and drama, gradually gained in popularity.

Pigeon fanciers were to be found in many streets in Rowley, their lofts a notable feature of backyards. Races were organised by such groups as the Worcestershire Federation, and prizes were eagerly fought over and treasured once won. At the start of the First World War pigeon racing stopped and the birds were 'called up' to the front to be used in carrying messages. One well-known venue for pigeon racers was the *Blue Ball* in Peartree Lane, Old Hill. Dog racing replaced dog fighting; Cradley Heath greyhounds ran just outside the borough at Dudley Wood, and brought in crowds from all over the West Midlands. A legendary breeder of Staffordshire Bull Terriers was Joe Mallen of the *Cross Guns* public house at Cradley Heath.

By 1850 a concert hall had been opened in Cradley Heath. Plays seem to have been mainly melodramas, but there were also magic shows and circus acts. At various times there were wild beast shows both in the open and in theatres, and, in particular, such entertainments were to be found at Rowley Wake in mid-September. Lions and tigers were exhibited in cages and sometimes performed 'tricks' with intrepid humans. Cradley Heath theatres, such as the Theatre Royal near Four Ways, staged comedy turns in the 1880s and 1890s, attracting local and national comedians, and it may have been in these theatres that the local characters of 'Anoch and Ali' (Enoch and Eli) gained popularity. Live theatre was slowly superseded by cinema, the first shows in Cradley Heath, according to the cinema historian Ned Williams, probably being given at a small building in Spinners End not far from the GWR goods yard.

The Empire is an example of a theatre being converted to cinema. Lying next to the *Hollybush Inn*, it had been opened on 11 September 1893 and was the meeting hall used by the striking chainmakers. In more recent memory the two best-known cinemas

137 *The ornate front and coat of arms on the former Rowley Regis Municipal Buildings, Old Hill.*

were the Royal and the Majestic. At the time of writing, the façade of the Royal in Bank Street, opened in 1912, still stands, despite many threats to demolish it. Cradley Heath's supercinema was the Majestic, opened on 27 March 1933. After the decline in film-going it became a bingo hall. Old Hill also had a cinema, the Grand, opened in 1913.

Ned Williams tells us that the first cinema in Blackheath was The Picture Palace, which was opened in July 1910. However, the first purpose-built cinema was The Pavilion in High Street. The Kings began to show films in 1923, with its own orchestra playing before the show. Blackheath's complement of cinemas later included The Rex and The Odeon, the latter part of a well-known Midland chain. Cinemas in Cradley Heath, Old Hill and Blackheath presented many hours of family entertainment and were the mainstay of popular dramatic experience from the 1910s to the 1960s. They made for a degree of social cohesion which was lost when television largely took over their role. However, it was after the 1960s put an end to so many cinemas that comedians such as Tommy Mundon and Dolly Allen developed

their Midland circuits with varieties of the 'Black Country Night Out'.

Traditional news media in Rowley Regis has been dominated by the Birmingham and Wolverhampton papers, but much local news was always carried by the Stourbridge-based *County Express*. A local enterprise covering all areas but Tividale was *The Circular*, which was masterminded by Mr Rollason and presented both news and reminiscences. This, too, was a factor for local homogeneity, as was the later *Black Country Bugle*, which covered an area much larger than Rowley Regis but included regular articles on the area. In this and other media one major interest has been dialect stories and poems.

The dialect of Rowley and of the Black Country generally is of great interest. Pronunciation, grammar and vocabulary have all shown, even in recent years, conservative features, many of which have vanished from nearby Birmingham, though 19th-century evidence suggests they were once present there too. The Orton-Deith dialect study of the 1960s omitted the area, but took vocabulary examples from Romsley in the old Halesowen parish which were identical with words used in Rowley. At this time an extensive traditional vocabulary was regularly used by a large proportion of the population; examples are manifold, but three random specimens are *tundish*, for a small culinary funnel, *nesh*, meaning weak in the face of a physical discomfort such as cold, and *glede* for a red-hot cinder.

In the late 20th century there were still speakers who preferred the 2nd person singular *'thee', 'thy', 'thine'* when addressing one person, and this was generally followed with the appropriate grammatical ending to the verb, e.g. *'thee cost'* for *'you can'*. The 3rd person plural ending in –n is also sometimes still heard, e.g. *'they 'an'* for *'they have'*. The verb *to be* shows traces of a regular conjugation: 'I bin, thee bist, he/she/it bin', but these are hardly ever heard nowadays except in parody or joke. Negatives without the letter T are still commonly heard: *'we co(r)'* for *'we can't'* seems to be short for *'we conna'*, the

negative implied by similar forms in White's *All Round the Wrekin* of 1860.

This conservative dialect is typical of much of the Black Country, but it has been especially tenacious in Rowley. The reason seems to be the parochial character of the villages in the 19th century, with population growth dependent on gradually increasing living standards, so that there was less need for emigration and immigration than in many areas of the country; as the industrial revolution continued, nail making gave way to chain making and quarrying to mining, then mining to a variety of industry, so that families could stay in the parish and borough. In a specimen area of the 1851 census (200 houses in Rowley Village) 77.5 per cent were born in Rowley, with a further 15 per cent born in adjoining parishes. Only 1.5 per cent came from outside the West Midlands. A slightly lower figure is found for Windmill End, but only in the Tividale portion of the

**138**   *Old Hill post office, Halesowen Road.*

census are there significant numbers of immigrants from other parts of Britain.

Concern about the vanishing character of the Black Country caused Dr John Fletcher of Bescot and John Brimble of Tipton to announce in December 1966 that they were to form a Black Country Society. This is region-wide but has stimulated great interest in Rowley Regis. It soon produced a regular programme, one of its early events being a celebration of so-called 'grorty' [groaty] pudding at the *Pear Tree Inn* at Rowley. The society's work has been enormously valuable, as the foremost amenity society of the whole West Midlands region; yet it is more than just an amenity society, fostering culture in all its forms, folk, popular and high. Much of its work is summed up in the quarterly magazine, *The Blackcountryman*, launched in 1967-8. A further 'spin-off' was the foundation of a museum, located in Dudley, now called the Black Country Living Museum, in which numerous old buildings from Rowley have been rebuilt.

Unlike the Potteries or Nottinghamshire, Birmingham and the Black Country have produced little literature. This has been even truer of Rowley, which has had no major fictional works located here. Francis Brett Young,

born in Halesowen, wrote novels, some of which include scenes set in 'Mawne' (Cradley Heath). *The Black Country Bugle* has provided space for short stories, often about ghosts or other horrors, by 'Aristotle Tump', and the *Birmingham Weekly Post* published short stories by E.R. Baker, which were collected, added to and published as *Black Country Stories* by Allen and Unwin in 1952. Some of these are very local, *Brewster's Revenge* being set in Tippity Green and Perry's Lake. These small masterpieces reflect the life of Rowley and district in the pre-war period. In 1973 Longman published a local ghost story, *Ghost in the Water*, set largely near Station Road, Old Hill, with Gorsty Hill Canal Tunnel given a fictional towpath though it was really a legging canal. The book was televised by the BBC in 1983.

Rowley was not well served in the 19th century by library and archive resources. In 1909 a gift was made by the Carnegie foundation which enabled libraries to be built at Blackheath, Cradley Heath and Tividale. Their opening was commemorated in the naming of Carnegie Road in Blackheath. They have remained small though efficient and friendly institutions, more recently developing IT and video services. Rowley Regis archives are scattered throughout the wider West Midlands, as appears from the bibliography at the end of this volume. Some interest in their collection was shown by the librarian J. Wilson-Jones in the 1950s, but he had little in the way of resources. He later wrote a book, *The History of the Black Country*, in which some earlier attempts at chronicling Rowley were re-presented.

Association football has been a major interest of Rowley people, mainly by their supporting West Bromwich Albion and Aston Villa, but other local teams such as Wolves have encouraged the wearing of scarves and

**139** *Advertisement for tonic drops for growing pigeons from the 1960s.*

## ROWLEY REGIS BRITANNIA PARK

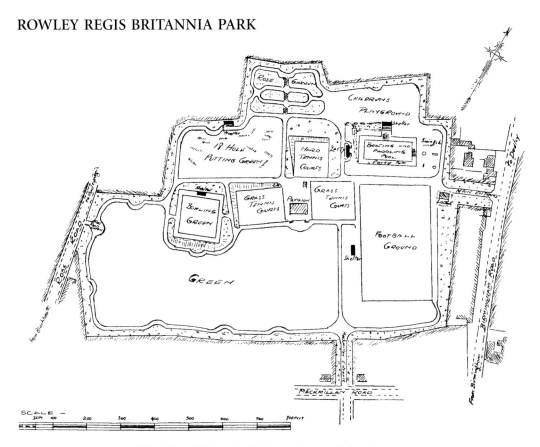

**140**  *Plan of Britannia Park from the souvenir brochure, 1932.*

shirts. Cradley Heath F.C. were Birmingham League champions in 1926/7 but there were many other local football teams, sometimes run by churches and chapels, such as the Rowley parish church team and the team run by St Luke's, Cradley Heath in the 1930s. More important on the regional and even national scene was Cradley Heath Speedway ('the Heathens'), whose first track parade was in July 1947 and who raced on the Dudley Wood ground, just outside the borough boundary. The team has had its ups and downs, and there is constant talk of its being reformed, but the problem of a suitable venue has not been solved at the time of writing.

In the south-east of the borough, High Harcourt, once the home of Alfred Barrs and a private school long known as 'Miss Harper's', provided space for what ultimately developed into Old Hill Tennis Club. However, many might consider the most prestigious sports club in Rowley to be Old Hill Cricket Club, who play on a superb ground at Haden Hill which seems far from the industrial Midlands and could be in the heart of Worcestershire. The club won the Birmingham League Championship, for example, in 1921, and produced the great Warwickshire and England bowler Eric Hollies. He was born in Halesowen Road in

**141** *Reddal Hill Carnegie Library.*

1912 and was carefully coached as a child by his bowler father, William. He began to play for Warwickshire in 1931 and was selected to tour the West Indies in 1934-5. During the Second World War first-class cricket was suspended and Eric played for Old Hill again, taking all ten wickets in a match against Mitchells and Butlers in 1940. He repeated the performance at county level in 1946, taking all ten wickets for 49 for Warwickshire against Nottinghamshire. He was chosen for the test team to tour Australia in 1950-1 and had many duels with Don Bradman and others.

In the late 19th century the piano was to be found in many respectable parlours in Rowley Regis. Chapel singing encouraged music-making, and the generation has only just died which enjoyed parlour ballads as well as such music hall songs as 'Don't go down the mine, Daddy', a song which is frequently the subject of enquiries in local papers. Traditional 'folk' songs were often sung, a splendid performer in this genre who

was captured on disc being George Dunn, who came from Quarry Bank but worked in his early life at the New British Iron Company's works. Among his repertoire, which included music hall songs and carols, were 'The cruel ship's carpenter', 'Cold blows the wind', 'Henry my son' (an old ballad, of which I have heard other versions in the neighbourhood), as well as early 20th-century songs such as 'Roses of Picardy'.

Much popular culture has centred on the public houses of Rowley, of which there are still a large number; they contrast with the vast roadhouses of the mid-20th century and the spruced up wine bars of later years. But beer has also been regularly brewed at home, in the 'brewhouse' across the yard. It is impossible to list these small pubs, though some illustrations are included; they have played a significant part in keeping the villages and small towns of Rowley parish attractive to the inhabitants, though many have followed the lamented *Old Hill Cross* into oblivion.

# XV

# Strikes, Wars and Local Government

The cholera outbreaks of 1832 and 1849 alerted central government to the fact that small parishes were struggling to regulate health in the burgeoning industrial towns, and as a result Local Boards of Health were created, one being at Rowley Regis, its bounds coterminous with the old parish. It relieved the Vestry from having to deal with health problems on a small poor rate. In 1871 Rowley Board of Health was succeeded by the Urban District Council. These councils had powers over such matters as fire and sanitation and Rowley Regis UDC offices were built behind Holy Trinity church. The fire station was at the west end of Trinity Schools and remarkably, though now converted into a shop, still displays the Rowley UDC logo at the time of writing. Until the 1902 Education Act schools were under the Rowley Regis School Board, but this was dissolved and powers were transferred to the UDC on 1 May 1903.

During the First World War many men of working age were recruited for the army, leaving services bereft. A 'Rowley Regis Company' of the Staffordshire Regiment was formed. Colliers and other key workers volunteered for service and this had an effect on the situation at home, a school log-book recording in January 1917 that there was only enough fuel for one fire and that the rest of the school was cold. Some teachers had also left, and others were employed at times to make out lists and do other clerking jobs. At Corngreaves School, five teachers were away at the war. The 150 territorials in possession of Powke Lane School during the summer holidays in 1915 brought their own military band.

The German enemy used Zeppelins to attack industrial targets in Britain. On 31 January 1916 the L21 appeared over Tividale, having mistaken the Black Country for Liverpool, thinking the canal was the Mersey. Tividale and Tipton had many industrial sites along the canal, and after dropping a bomb on Tipton the Zeppelin headed for Bradley, Bilston and Wednesbury, where further bombs were dropped. Walsall was the next target, after which the airship moved on to Sutton Coldfield and was then seen near Nuneaton, finally bombing a blast furnace in Northamptonshire.

The women chainmakers made headlines with their strike in 1910, although this was not the only industrial dispute by a long way, and their efforts resulted in the founding in 1912 of the Workers' Institute in Lomey Town. Industrial relations in Rowley were not the worst in the Black Country and Chartism had never become centred here, but nevertheless, as we have seen, bad times for the owners resulted in worse for the workers. The Haden family, represented by the Haden-Bests and then by the Bassanos, knew what they owed the community in return for the ruined landscape and poverty, and Bassano gave financial support to the building of Holy Trinity, Old Hill, in 1876 while G.A.H. Haden-Best paid £9,000 to build Trinity Schools in Halesowen Road, a fine lofty building which lasted until 1971.

One major cause of complaint against coal owners was subsidence. This was illustrated graphically when in February 1914 there was a major collapse in Cradley Heath, caused by the Stour Colliery at the rear of the defunct New British Iron Company's works. This had been closed by Lord Dudley, but re-leased and perilously re-opened by a Mr David Parsons. In his *Cradley Heath, Old Hill and District* Ron Moss describes the noises heard the night before, the ominous creakings and the sound of walls cracking. Bricks fell out of walls and next morning it was discovered that a large portion of High Street had disappeared, leaving the tram lines clear of the surface. Typically, though an enquiry took place, no criminal charges were brought. In some ways the High Street was lucky, for reconstruction took place at once; many properties in the Rowley area remained leaning or held together with iron ties after mining subsidence.

Pits in Rowley were being worked out or flooded owing to the inability of owners to agree on a comprehensive drainage scheme. By 1901 Waterfall Lane, Black Waggon and Old Lion in Old Hill were all closed, leaving 'pit bonks' (banks) behind them. Higher up the hill Scotwell had also closed, but in Rowley itself Bell End and Rowley Hall were still working. North of the hills, Tividale, Denbigh Hall and Groveland were all finished, but Lye Cross continued to flourish. The writing was

on the wall for Rowley Regis collieries and in 1920 there was a strike, the successor to many. (In 1884 children had been kept off school to go picking coal from the pit 'bonks'.) The 1920 strike was temporarily settled but renewed in April 1921. In the aftermath of the war the miners felt justified in pressing their claims for a standard country-wide wage but, given the precarious situation in Old Hill and Rowley, this did not suit the owners.

The strike was answered with a State of Emergency. No coal was being produced, which meant that the mine pumping engines had no fuel. Old Hill collieries were flooded despite great pumps having been installed at the foot of Waterfall Lane. Water rose in all the mines and soon was near the top of the shafts. Many miles of workings were under water. In the circumstances everyone suffered: the colliers on strike, the traders with no customers, the homes with no heat. Trinity Schools were used for a meeting to organise 'soup kitchens', cheap ways of feeding the starving children of miners and others. Coal picking on pit mounds was again prevalent, and miners assembled in hundreds to protest and support the pickers, for the pit banks were also being explored by the mine owners, desperate to supply customers, and removing what had been waste coal, slack and other stuff of rejected quality, was illegal.

By May 1921 there were major clashes between carters and miners. Three hundred colliers forced carters to empty out their wagons of picked coal, then climbed the hills to Pennant Hill Colliery behind Hawes Lane and forced the carters there to drop their loads. Tempers frayed and there were assaults on police and carters. By mid-May there were almost 10,000 unemployed men in Cradley Heath, but the strike was eventually brought to an end in July, when the miners accepted a

142    *Rowley Regis Endowed School Mission Hall in the 1950s.*

pay cut. Rowley coal mines never recovered, and small attempts made later to reopen old pits or mine opencast coal proved ineffective. The final blow was the 1926 national strike, when 6,000 people in Rowley were on strike in various industries, buses were immobilised by removing tyre valves, and there were violent clashes with volunteers and other non-striking workmen. Politically, Rowley Regis was often Labour-controlled, though combined Liberal/Conservative council candidates frequently succeeded.

A large area containing the industrial and residential towns of Cradley Heath, Old Hill, Blackheath and Tividale could not remain a UDC, and the movement to allow Rowley to become a borough eventually succeeded. A charter was granted in 1933, parades being held in celebration on 28 September of that year, and at Tividale the MP George Lansbury, leader of the Labour Party, celebrated the occasion with the new town clerk, Clifford Buckley. Rowley Borough was to last for just over thirty years but ambitious plans were afoot, and in 1937 fine new municipal

buildings were opened at the south-west end of Old Hill, opposite Beauty Bank and near to Haden Hill.

The ancient hall at Haden Hill had been supplemented in 1876 with an extension, and the old hall declined in use. Nomenclature for the old house and its extension have never been fully standardised, and there is sometimes confusion over which building is being referred to. In earlier days the hall was apparently called Hill Purlieu, or often just 'the house'. More recently the old hall has been called 'the Hall' and the Victorian addition 'Haden Hill House'. When George Alfred Haden-Best died in 1921 the whole property was put up for sale and the UDC decided to try to buy it. After some doubt a public meeting agreed to set up a fund, and the halls and park were bought on 14 October 1922 for the people of Rowley Regis. Britannia Park at Blackheath, with a pool which had once been the farm pond at Stilehouse, opened on 9 April 1932, and Tividale Park, once part of the grounds of Tividale Hall, opened on 3 October 1927.

The old hall at Haden Hill was in a precarious condition, and it was suggested in 1934 that it should be demolished. There was a public outcry, but £2,000 for its restoration was deemed too much for ratepayers to pay. Nevertheless, after intervention by A.M. Bassano and others, the hall was saved for the time being. Haden Hill Park and the surrounding area were well maintained and they have survived to the present time but there was more trouble to come for the hall itself.

Two years after the Municipal Buildings opened the country was again at war. Young men were again recruited for the services, leaving factories and chain-shops staffed by women or older men. 'Home Guard' platoons were formed, affiliated to the South Staffordshire Regiment, and air-raid shelters were constructed in school playgrounds. By 1940

they were in use, though raids were mainly at night. In late August there were all-night raids during which the old Birmingham Market Hall in the city centre was burnt down. In November bombs fell in Rowley borough, one of them, a land-mine, striking Grace Mary Estate at Upper Tividale, damaging a large number of houses and killing up to fifteen people. On 20 December 1940 two similar land-mines fell just over the boundary in Quarry Bank. Children were issued with gas masks to be carried to school every day, but there were heavy snowfalls, and in January 1941 schools were closed because air-raid shelters could not be used.

Rowley Regis adopted a destroyer, HMS *Tumult*, for which collections were made in works and schools. The ship captured a German flag which was then shown around the borough. Another wartime effort was 'Wings for Victory', for which Beeches Road school together with Siviter's Lane and Powke Lane organised a 'mile of pennies' which were laid down in the road and people were then asked to contribute to make the line longer. Rowley Regis sponsored a Castle Bromwich-built Spitfire. Small garden plots were planted with vegetables in a 'Dig for Victory' campaign. Money was also collected for the Prisoners of War fund.

The war with Germany eventually ended on 7 May 1945. Schools closed for two days and there were street parties such as the one organised at Surfeit Hill, Cradley Heath, by Mr and Mrs Frank Chapman and Mr and Mrs Reg Clarke. High hopes for a cleaner Black Country were raised after the war and a landmark was the publication in 1948 of *Conurbation*, a plan for the whole of the Birmingham and Black Country area. This gave the 1939 population of Rowley Regis as 44,780 and the total acreage of private and public open space as 320, less than

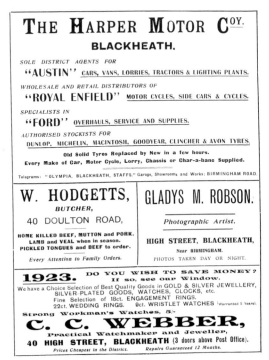

*143 Advertisements for Blackheath and Rowley Regis businesses in 1923.*

Oldbury but more than Tipton or Wednesbury. Included was the Dudley golf course at Turner's Hill, which with derelict land still provides a space clear of building at the geographical centre of Rowley Regis. Among the recommendations of the plan was the provision of much more open space through purchase of private land and refurbishment of old industrial scars.

Provision of council houses had begun before the war, and by the end of the 1950s there was a series of well-laid-out estates, chief among which were Brickhouse, Blackheath, Station Road, Old Hill, Codsall and roads at Upper Tividale, including Grace Mary Estate. New private housing was built at High Haden and on small plots in other areas, along the Birmingham New Road at Tividale, to the west of Old Hill and in parts of Blackheath. Rowley was represented by MP Arthur Henderson (Labour), who kept a close eye on his constituency and was noted for taking groups of schoolchildren round the Houses of Parliament. After much upheaval it looked as if the borough now had a settled future. But by the mid-1960s, clouds indicating a further change began to gather.

**BETTY BIRD**

(Late A. Suckling, Market Hall, B'ham)

High Class Floristry
Artistic Designs

69, Birmingham Road, Blackheath

THOMAS GADD

Ross Rivet Works
Rowley Regis
NEAR BIRMINGHAM

'Phone : Blackheath 1020

*Telegrams:*
Thomas Gadd, Rowley Regis

J. ADAMS

LADIES' & GENT'S
HIGH CLASS
**Hairdressing**

156 HIGH ST., BLACKHEATH
BIRMINGHAM

'Phone : Blackheath 1781

**THE VILLAGE FISH SHOP**

FRESH FISH DAILY          FRIED FISH & CHIPS

**D. Bennett,**
**37, High Street, Rowley Regis**

144  *Advertisements for Blackheath and Rowley Regis businesses in 1953.*

# XVI

# Reorganisation and After

In the 1960s the West Midlands, like other conurbations, contained a jumble of different kinds of administration in close geographical proximity. Rowley was among a number of small boroughs which seemed anomalous set against larger towns like Birmingham and Wolverhampton. It was felt that the resources available to the larger places should be shared with the smaller ones, and this could be done by amalgamating boroughs. Smethwick and Oldbury had co-operated in the past and shared various facilities, and in 1966 it was decided that Rowley should join them in a new county borough to be called Warley, after a small area in the south of the district, and to be included in Worcestershire. Rowley was back in the old county, but not for long, for the reaction among most Rowley residents was dismay. The new borough was described as 'Warley white elephant', and it was claimed with some justification that Smethwick, a county borough, would be able to rule the new entity without opposition.

The feelings of people in Old Hill and Blackheath were voiced by the Independent councillors J.W. and J. Shakespeare in their interim report to electors in October 1966:

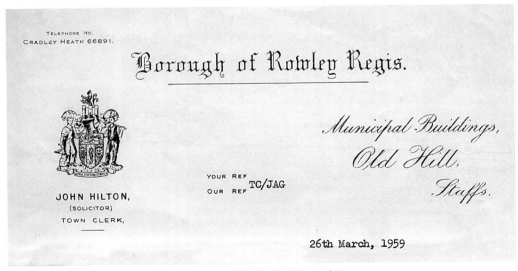

145  *Letterhead of Rowley Regis borough in 1959.*

146 *Advertisement for Repetition Metal Products, 1950s. Machines had taken over handmade production.*

147 *On a Black Country Society Christmas card, typical Black Country workmen see the three kings arriving in an idealised Midlands.*

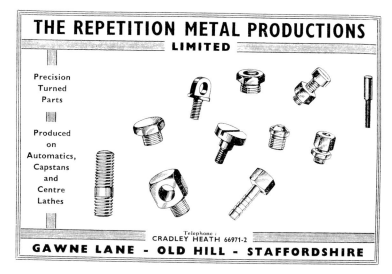

**THE REPETITION METAL PRODUCTIONS**
LIMITED

Precision Turned Parts

Produced on Automatics, Capstans and Centre Lathes

Telephone :
CRADLEY HEATH 66971-2

**GAWNE LANE - OLD HILL - STAFFORDSHIRE**

'There are … some very expensive housing schemes in Smethwick, which … will have to be paid for in part by Old Hill and Blackheath people'; 'There are more than 30 committees and sub-committees. When their reports … come before the council … there is an attitude of antagonism instead of a business-like get-together'; 'Offices and officers are scattered and in turmoil.' Some of these problems were the natural growing pains of a new authority, but they also resulted in part from the attempt to link together incompatible places. However, all the participants would have been surprised to know that the new arrangement would last only six years before another reorganisation hit the region in 1972. (See also fig.127 on p.105.)

This time a West Midlands County was created, although most of its functions would later be abolished. Hapless Rowley, along with Oldbury and Smethwick, was this time joined with West Bromwich, Tipton and Wednesbury in a new 'metropolitan' borough to be named Sandwell after a small area on the West Bromwich/Handsworth boundary miles from Rowley Regis, of which few people had heard. Welding together the disparate parts of the new borough would be a major task and is not over even yet. In 2004-5 there was a failed movement to re-name the borough West Bromwich, and there are frequent wrangles about signposting for 'Sandwell', which has no centre and whose offices are scattered in various towns.

Under Warley, new council housing was built at Riddings Mound in Old Hill and elsewhere. (The Riddings Mound tower blocks were spectacularly blown up and demolished when tall flats became unfashionable.) The abolition of the Oldbury/Rowley border allowed a new school, St Michael's, to be built at Throne Road which took pupils from Lion Farm and from the Oldbury side of the hills. The then GPO decided to rationalise postal district names and lose the separate addresses of Old Hill and Blackheath, calling these places parts of Cradley Heath and Rowley Regis respectively. But part of the old

borough was given a postcode prefix B for Birmingham and part DY for Dudley, and there was an outcry over the 'abolition' of Old Hill and Blackheath, which Sandwell Council eventually remedied by erecting signs at the entrance to the towns. It was decided that High Street, Old Hill should become Highgate Street to distinguish it from Cradley Heath High Street so that there would not be two High Streets in the same postcode area.

This final chapter could easily become a litany of demolition, but one amazing success has been the retention and restoration of Haden Hall, which had been decaying during wartime and after. Despite the brave words of J. Wilson-Jones, who hoped it would become a museum, it was used as little more than the back-drop for wedding photographs. In the mid-1960s further plans to demolish it were announced, but a group was formed to fight the proposal, which was able to have the hall

**148**  *Mary Macarthur Park, Lomey Town, Cradley Heath.*

149 *Form 4a at Beeches Road (Highfields) School in 1956. Back row, left to right: Pauline Temple, Kathleen Knowles, Jennifer Hadley, Cynthia Turner, Christine Johns, Margaret Smith, Carolyn Cockin, Susan Holden, Diane Cole, Sheila Downing, Janet Parkes, Jean Davies, Pauline Wood: third row: Brian Carter, Gay Wooley, Irene Johnson, Dilys Parkes, Valerie Jones, Muriel Cox, Margaret Hollingsworth, Beryl Barnsley, Joan Gardner, Joan Bryan, Janet Smith, Douglas Masterson: second row: Lorna Dallow, Kathleen Phillips, Glenys Williams, Pat Witts, Christine Westwood, Diana Beatrup, Mr Horace Wilson, Tommy Groves, Kenneth Taylor, Michael Guise, ?, ?, Roy Sherwood: front row: Peter Bird, Colin Adams, John Horton, Trevor Chandler, Kenneth Darby, Keith Balmer, Edward Rhoden, ?, Kenneth Williams, Roger Barnett.*

opened for rare conducted visits, when such relics as the 17th- or 18th-century windows and the alleged secret passage to Halesowen Abbey (probably in fact a drain) were shown. Enough money was raised to allow emergency roof repairs and the council drew back from the demolition proposal. With grants from English Heritage and other bodies, the hall is now undergoing total restoration, which should ensure its future.

This was not to be the fate of historic but undermined Portway Hall, once home to the Russells and later to the recalcitrant Daniel Johnson. It was demolished in 1979,

leaving a strange parody of itself in the shape of a newer house just round the corner in Throne Road. The site of Warren's Hall, with its moat, is now hard to distinguish, but better luck befell Corngreaves Hall, which passed into council ownership and has been renovated. More widespread still has been the demise and demolition of major industrial complexes, such as Doulton's pottery works, closed in 1979, and Dudley and Dowell's ironfounders at Cradley Heath. Chain-shops also are a thing of the past.

Whole areas have changed their characters completely. Tividale is almost

**150**   *Warren's Hall Park, looking towards the restored engine house.*

unrecognisable, with many new roads of 1980s and 1990s houses leading off Dudley Road. Rowley Village and Hawes Lane were the subject of a major demolition programme begun in the early 1970s to make way for a road-widening scheme which was never carried out. The Conservative Club is almost the only remaining Victorian building in Hawes Lane, such interesting buildings as the Methodist church (demolished in 1973) and Prospect House, with its Regency portico, succumbing to the need for a new road which did not materialise. The houses and cottages on the south-west side of Rowley Village disappeared completely, together with most of those on the east side, including the Georgian house with its Rowley stone arch and acorn gateposts. By-passes at Blackheath and Old Hill caused demolition of many rows of dwellings.

Cradley Heath open market was renowned for many years as a place to find bargains. It was closed and in 1969 a new covered market was opened, which still houses stalls where bargains may be snapped up. At Blackheath market, the road layout was redesigned to replace the underground toilets with a green traffic island. Road widening took place at Whiteheath, and the Halesowen Road at Old Hill beyond Haden Hill was tidied up; speed limits changed according to the prevailing view on this issue. Many new houses and flats have been built where old roads have gone, at Cherry Orchard (demolished in 1970) for example, as well as multi-storey flats such as those at Riddings Mound and across former waste land at 'The Quack' near Rowley Hall. Chapels, pubs and schools have also closed or, in some cases, been rebuilt.

**151**  *The canal at Tividale, showing the entrance to an old canal basin which no longer serves a local factory.*

**152**  *Cradley Heath station in 2005. A ten-minute service now operates to Stourbridge and Birmingham.*

**153**   *The entrance to Old Hill in 2005, showing a district sign and the disused Wesleyan Methodist church.*

**154**   *The Balaji Temple in Tividale is one of many new worship buildings erected by new communities in Rowley Regis.*

A highly successful project was the development of Warren's Hall Country Park, on land below Dudley Road which had previously been part farm land and partly derelict after the closure of the Warren's Hall and Windmill End collieries. This involved the restoration of Cobbs Engine House, the former pumping station for Windmill End colliery which was built in 1831 to pump, with another one at Waterfall Lane, water from mines. It has a splendid chimney 95ft tall; and the gable of the main building is 26ft high. It is thought that the engine was originally a low pressure engine but was modified in 1874 and 1910. Renovation work began in 1974 after a gift of £8,000 from Warley Council. The lane nearby and the fields on which the engine stands are called Cobbs on the 1800 map, but no one of this name has been found in the area so it is unlikely that Cobbs Engine House is named after a local farmer; it is more likely to be a shortened version of 'copyhold', since this area was copyhold land.

Warren's Hall Park also takes in the mouth of the Netherton Tunnel (1858), the last canal tunnel to be built, furnished with lighting and two towpaths. One of the few brooks in Rowley which has not radically changed course or been dispersed after the mining operations of the 19th century runs here, from a pool which existed before the Warren's Hall pits were opened. This pool and the Dudley No.2 Canal, which also runs through the site, are quiet haunts of fishermen, though the pool formerly near Warren's Hall farmhouse (not the same as the old hall) was drained in 1988.

Sports facilities in the area were enhanced by the opening of Haden Hill Leisure Centre, with a fine swimming pool replacing that at the side of Haden Hill Park. The former Municipal Buildings are still in council

155   *Advertisement by the West Bromwich Building Society showing a No. 87 tram.*

use as the headquarters of the Buildings Department. Britannia Park lost its boating pool in common with other places, as health and safety rules made such pools difficult to guard and keep clean. The Black Country Living Museum has taken on the role of preserving of Rowley heritage, putting on show such industrial relics as Lench's oliver shop, moved there in 1977.

As Rowley Regis has become a collection of commuting towns, better transport has become imperative. Since the opening of the Jewellery Line a ten-minute service has gradually been developed from both Cradley Heath and Rowley Regis stations, trains going via Birmingham to Solihull or Stratford in one direction and Kidderminster and Worcester in the other. A through service to London from Cradley Heath has been operated by Chiltern Lines.

Shopping throughout the West Midlands has been much affected by the opening of Merry Hill Centre between Brierley Hill and Quarry Bank. New shops were built at Old Hill after the demolition of Trinity Schools, and Blackheath High Street shops still retain solid custom, but small corner shops have on the whole disappeared, and outlets included in designs for post-war estates such as at Rowley Hall have mostly closed. Cradley Heath attracts local shoppers with a wide range of businesses, some national but some still local. There are new house agents to cater for the increasing numbers of private houses being built on small plots throughout the former borough. It is possible that the future of Rowley Regis is mainly as a series of dormitory towns for the offices and services in Merry Hill, Dudley and Birmingham.

# Select Bibliography

**Printed materials**

Auden, Miss, *Rowley Regis Parish Register*, Staffs Parish Register Society, 1912-15
*Black Country Bugle, The*
*Blackcountryman, The*
*Blackheath Junior and Infant Schools*, 1979
'Britain in old photographs' series, especially volumes by Ron Moss and Anthony H. Page
Broadbent, R.C., *Burnt Tree Round and About*, 1983
Burritt, E., *Walks in the Black Country and its Green Borderland*, London, 1868
*Haden Hill Park*, a brochure, including extracts from 'an account of the family of de la Hauede, by Charles Walter Bassano', 1934
*Historical Collections for Staffordshire*, 1928, 1936 etc
Jones, J. Wilson, *The History of the Black Country*, Cornish Brothers Ltd, nd
*Kelly's Post Office Directory of Birmingham*, etc., 1860
Rollason, A., *The Ancient Manor of Rowley Regis*, Dudley Herald, 1921
Rowley Regis St Giles parish magazine, BRL 389513
Souvenir of the opening of the Rowley Regis Britannia Park, 1932
Webb, J. S., *Black Country Tramways*, Bloxwich, 1976
*White's Directory*, 1834
White, W., *All round the Wrekin*, London, 1860
Williams, Ned, *Cinemas of the Black Country*, 1982

**Manuscript sources**

(BRL Birmingham Reference Library; SRO Staffordshire Record Office; WRO Worcestershire Record Office)
Censuses 1841 and 1851, National Archives
Churchwardens' Presentments, Faculties, Consistory Court Records, WRO
Deeds relating to Hedger's Mill, WRO 2422/21
Deeds relating to Tividale Hall, SRO 285/M//T/1-30
Deeds relating to Portway Farm, SRO D 364 M 293

Deeds relating to land in Rowley Village, BRL 338264
Deeds of the Dudley family (court rolls, etc.), Dudley Archives
Deeds relating to Darby's Farm, Dudley Archives, bundle 16/2
Deeds relating to land at Tividale in Rowley Somery, BRL 337361, 337367
Deeds relating to sale of a cottage in Rowley Regis, 1693 BRL 234432-3
Jameson Documents, BRL deposit no. 7384L
List of Lord Dudley's tenants (1819), WRO 9346
Pedigree of Turton family, BRL 317303
Petition against rebuilding of church, 1812, Rowley Parish Church
Plan of Rowley Somery c.1850, private collection
Reference to the plan of the Parish of Rowley Regis, c.1800
Rowley Regis Vestry minute books and Select Vestry minute books, formerly
    Rowley Parish Church, now Sandwell Archives
Rowley Regis Inclosure Award and plan, SRO
Rowley Regis parish plan, BRL
Rowley Regis wills, 1560-1729, WRO
Rowley Regis wills, National Archives (PCC wills)
Typescript on Grainger's Lane, from Mr Wilson Woodhouse
Unattributed diaries supplied by A.B. Smith, Vicky Homer (maiden name)

# Index

Act of Uniformity 22
Addenbrook family 13, 17,
Allsop's Hill 63
Aston 52
Aston Villa 114
Attwood family 43, 49, 59, 61
Auden (Allden) family 40, 43
Aynsworth family 23, 92

Badger, T & I 51
Baker, E.R. 114
Bannister family 74, 100
Baptist churches 97, 100-1
Barehill 29
Barnsley family 69, 70
Barrs, George 2, 26, 44, 47, 50-1, 59, 90,
    92, 100-1, 111
Barrs Road (Pig Lane) 49, 59
Bassano family 96, 118
Bate family 30, 43, 65, 92
Bearmore 11, 43
Beeches Road, 101, 120, 125
Beet, John 43, 49-50
Bell End 16, 87, 101, 118
Billingham family 74, 100
Bilston 45, 117
Birmingham 15, 22, 38-9, 47, 49, 60, 71,
    72, 78, 80, 88, 89, 92, 95-6, 100, 103,
    105, 112, 120, 122, 124, 127, 129-30
Bissell family 40
*Black Country Bugle, The* 112
Black Country character 72, 114
Black Country dialect 112-3
Black Country Living Museum 80, 114,
    129
Black Country Society 114, 123
*Blackcountryman, The* 114
Black Waggon colliery 51, 53, 118
Blackheath 16, 41-2, 51, 55, 71, 77, 79,
    81, 87, 89, 92, 95, 101-2, 104, 112, 114,
    119-22, 124, 126
*Blue Ball, The* (Tividale) 32
Blue Bell farm (Bryfield) 34, 36
Bowater family 101
Brades 11, 16, 20, 23, 32, 39, 43, 45, 52, 59,
    61, 62, 69, 81, 92, 97
Brett Young, Francis 84, 114
Brickhouse 19, 21, 23, 30, 52, 54, 56, 63
Brick making 64, 65-6, 69
Bridg(e)water family 19, 38, 50
Brierley Hill 45, 81, 105, 108
Brimble, John 114
Brindley, James 57
*Britannia Inn, see* Stilehouse

Britannia Park 16, 115, 119, 129
British Iron Company and Works 52
Bromsgrove 29, 34, 71
*Bull's Head, The* (Tippity Green) 55
Burn hill, 52
Burnt Tree 81
Burritt, Elihu 61-2, 65, 69, 72
Bus services 80, 89

Cakemore 4
Camp Hawes and Camp House 8, 18
Canal, Dudley No. 2 40, 51, 58, 69, 129
Canals 39ff, 45
Cartwright family 17, 19
Chain making 73-6, 111, 117, 125
Chambers family 30
Chapman family 120
Cheverton, F.C. 90, 94, 104
Cholera 50, 117
Cinemas 111-12
*Circular, The* 112
City Road, Tividale, 16, 26, 83, 89, 110
Clarke family 95, 120
Clent 4, 7, 9, 26, 38, 42
Club Buildings 41, 101
Coal mining 45, 52-4, 66, 67, 75, 118-9
'Cobbs' engine house 85, 129
Cock Green and *The Cock* 46
Colborne family 18, 24, 97
Compton Return 24, 97
Corngreaves 16, 43, 49, 53, 59, 64, 86, 103,
    108, 117
Corngreaves Furnace Co. 61
Corngreaves Hall 42-3, 59, 61, 125
*County Express, The* 94
Cradley 2, 13, 21, 79, 97, 100
Cradley Forge 21, 30, 34
Cradley Heath 6, 18, 23, 30, 34, 42, 51-2,
    59, 70, 74-8, 80, 84, 89, 92, 98, 100-2,
    109, 111-2, 114-5, 118-9, 124-7, 129
Cricket 115-6
Crowley family 23
Crump, William 92

Danks family 52
Darby family 17, 51
Darby's Hill 65, 86, 102
Dawes, William 51
Derrett's Hall *see* Tividale Hall
Dobb's Bank 23, 35
Doulton's pottery 86, 125
Downing family 43
Dudley 2, 7, 11, 16, 18, 34, 48, 50, 71, 73,
    75, 78, 80, 84, 88-9, 104, 108, 121,

124, 130
Dudley, Lord 11, 17, 19, 48, 69, 75, 103, 118
Dudley Wood 74, 111, 115
Dunn, George 116

Edwards family 36
Eld, Francis 49
Enclosure Act and Award 42ff, 59, 99
Endowed School 87, 104
Erdington 21

Fereday, Joseph 52
Five Ways, Cradley Heath 98, 102
Flavell, Joshua 49
Fletcher, Dr John 114
Foley family 99
Folk songs 116
Football 114-5
Four Ways, Cradley Heath 100, 111
Fox Oak 34, 74
Foxall, Mary 45

Gaunt family 29, 34, 38, 40, 43
Gawne 52, 71
Giles, Edward 47
Gones, George 70
Gorsty Hill 40, 47, 101
Grace Mary Estate and colliery 86, 120-1
Grainger, Daniel 74
Grainger's Lane 99, 100, 109
Greyhound racing 111
Grove family 17, 32, 49
Groveland (Grovelands) 15, 18, 22, 31, 57,
    85, 97, 118
Gun barrel works 69
Gunpowder Plot 19, 50
Gypsy Lane *see* City Road

Hackett family 46, 51
Haden Cross 15, 96
Haden family 13, 17-8, 23-4, 28-9, 34, 41,
    43-4, 91, 94, 96-7, 106, 118
Haden Hill 13, 15, 19, 23, 26-7, 34, 44, 56,
    65, 86, 106, 115, 119-20, 124-6, 129
Hadley family 69
Hailstone, 4, 29, 64, 65, 85
Halesowen 2, 6-7, 35, 40, 72, 73, 78,7 9, 96
Halesowen Abbey 11, 14, 17, 125
Hall Lane 32
Hancox, Benjamin 74
Harborne 6, 89
Hart's Tenement 30
Hawes Lane 1, 37-8, 65, 67, 101, 105-6, 126
Hayseech 43, 69, 73, 99

Hedger's Mill 21, 23, 34
Hickman & Wright 51
Higgs family 51
High Street (Highgate Street) Old Hill 16
Higham's Hill 4, 23, 65
Hill, Thomas 48
Hingley, Noah 52, 55, 74
Holcroft & Pearson 51
Hollies, Eric 115
Holy Trinity church, Old Hill 96, 101, 117-8
Holyoak, George 29
Hunt family 20, 43, 52, 59, 61

Iron production 59-62

'Jewellery Line' 79
Jews' harps 70
Johnson family 45, 125
Jones, John 52

Keir, James 40, 43, 51
Kendrick family 75
King's Norton 7
Kings cinema 112
Kingswinford 6, 7, 71
Knowle 11, 23, 51-2, 64, 93, 104-5

Latin place name 7-8
Lench's, 'Excelsior Works' 83
Lion Tube Works 60
Liverpool 74
Lloyd, George T. 108-10
Lomey Town 74, 104
Longbridge 79
Lowe family 98
Lye Cross, Upper Tividale 16, 65, 102, 118
Lyttelton, Lord 35

Macarthur, Mary 75
Macefields 104, 107
Mackmillan family and trust 37, 40-1, 92, 98, 103, 105-6
Meryhurst 7
Methodism and Methodist churches 73, 87, 93, 98-102, 126, 128
Midland Red buses 78, 80, 81, 83, 89
Mincing Lane 9, 16, 23
Mineral railways 49, 51, 82, 86
Mining subsidence 118
Monins family 23, 26-7, 35, 38, 91, 103
Moor Lane 6, 18
Moore, John 91
Moss, Ron 75-6, 118
Mushroom Green (Musham or Mursham) 74-5

Nail making 71ff.
Neptune, The 63
Netherton 40, 55, 59, 74, 84, 97
Netherton Canal Tunnel 2, 129
New British Iron Company 59, 60-1, 64, 86, 103, 116, 118
Newby, Thomas 92
Newtown 69, 74
Nicklin family 31
Nock family 48-9, 52, 95
Northfield 40, 71, 79, 89, 95

Oakham(formerly Holcum and Holcombe) 7, 23, 29-31
Odeon cinema 112
Old Hill 1, 6, 15-6, 34, 36, 43, 51-3, 58, 61, 63, 65-6, 69-75, 76-81, 84-5, 92, 94-6, 100-2, 104-5, 108, 112-24, 126, 128, 130

Old Lion colliery 51, 118
Oldbury 2, 6-7, 16, 31, 71, 77, 81, 88, 121-4
Orme family 17, 19-20, 40

Parkes family 17, 20, 23, 92, 100
Parsons family 45, 73
Pavilion cinema 112
Payton family 92
Penhouse 34
Penn 20, 29
Pensnett 45, 89
Perry's Lake 68, 69, 114
Perry Park Road 81
Piddock's Green 98
Pigeon racing 111, 113
Pittaway, Thomas 71
Plant family and Plant Street 30-1, 95, 103
Politics 119
Poor Law, 50
Portway 2, 28, 32, 34, 45, 51, 65
Portway Hall 11, 22-4, 43, 54, 64
Powke Lane 11, 15, 20, 104-6, 117

Quarry Bank 2, 71, 116, 120, 130
Quarrying 43, 63ff, 68, 70
Quinton 89, 94, 96, 99

Railways 60, 69, 77-82, 86, 100, 127, 129
Ramrod Hall 69
Raybould family 36, 90
Reddal Hill 38, 43, 49, 70, 75, 92, 95-6, 98, 100, 103-4, 106-7, 116
Rex cinema 112
Riddings Mound 1, 124
Rolinson/Rollinson family 43, 45
Ross 71
Rough Hill 65
Round family 45, 52, 111
Rowley Church bells 24, 32
Rowley Hall 13, 16, 19, 23-4, 32, 43, 48, 49-50, 56, 65, 92, 118, 126
Rowley Parish Church (St Giles') 10-11, 14, 19, 40, 44, 48, 70, 89, 90ff
Rowley ragstone 6, 63-5, 90, 92
Rowley Regis Grammar School 67, 104-9
Rowley Regis manor 9, 42
Rowley Regis UDC 81, 117
Rowley Somery 8-9, 11, 19, 23, 25, 29, 42
Rowley Village 6, 16, 27, 32-3, 36, 40, 48, 50-2, 63, 70-1, 77, 80, 86, 98, 100-1, 103-4, 113, 126
Rushton/Ruston family 23, 101
Russell family 11, 17, 23, 91, 125
Russell's Hall fault 52

St Giles' church, see Rowley Parish Church
St James chapel ('rhubarb chapel') 101
St Luke's church 45, 85, 91, 93, 95, 99, 109, 115
St Michael's church, Tividale 96
St Paul's church, Blackheath 96
Salvation Army 102
Sandwell and Sandwell Metropolitan Borough 2, 123-4
Saunders, Thomas 28-9
Sedgley Beacon 2
Shakespeare family 84-5, 105, 122
Shenstone, William 35
Sidaway family 34, 38, 70, 92, 98, 100
Siviter's Lane 32, 36, 63, 98, 104-5
Slack Hillock 52
Smethwick 6, 78, 81, 83, 122
Speedway 115
Spring Meadow 100-1

Springfield 39, 85
Stafford, Marquis of 42-3, 48
Station Road, Old Hill 40, 58
Stebbing Shaw 40-1
Stilehouse (Stylehouse) 35, 98, 103
Stour river 7, 16, 21, 34
Stourbridge 6, 79, 100, 112, 127
Sunday school processions 102
Sutton Coldfield 48, 117

Taylor family 40, 54
Temple Meadow, see Wright's Lane
Theatres 111
Thompson family 50, 52
Tibbetts family 99
Tibbett's Gardens 74, 99
Tilley family 98
Tinsley, Eliza 76
Tippity Green 30, 43, 45, 55, 63, 114
Tipton 2, 7, 31, 39, 51, 59, 77, 105, 108, 117, 121, 123
Tithes 42
Tividale 2, 6, 8, 15-6, 18, 26, 39-40, 43, 51, 52, 57, 65, 77, 82, 83, 86, 95, 98, 101, 104, 108, 110, 112-4, 117-21, 127-8
Tividale Hall 14-5, 22, 26-7, 38-9, 51, 83, 98
Tommy shops 62
Totnal 15, 34, 51
Trade Unions 75, 117
Tramways (passenger) 77, 79, 80-1, 83
'Tump,' The 81
Turner's Hill 2, 6, 16, 26-7, 32, 43, 50, 63, 65, 102
Turton family 17, 20, 22, 28, 32, 91, 92, 97

Walsall 15, 117
Warley 92, 94, 105, 124, 129
Warren's Hall 12-13, 43, 56, 59, 82, 86, 125, 129
Waterfall Lane 11, 20, 23, 53, 60, 88, 118, 129
Watts, Isaac 101
Wednesbury 52, 117, 121, 123
Weoley Castle 47
Wesley, John 99
West Bromwich 17, 19-20, 22, 83, 89, 91, 123, 129
West Bromwich Albion 114
West Midlands County 123
White family 19, 92
White, Walter 71, 72, 112
Whiteheath 15, 18, 43, 47, 126
Whitehouse family 50
Willetts family 18, 23, 34
Williams, Ned 111
Wilson-Jones, J. 114, 124
Windmill End 11, 16, 23, 40, 52, 67, 80, 113, 129
Withymoor 52, 67
Wolverhampton 39, 72, 88, 89, 112, 122
Wolverhampton 'New' Road 88-9, 121
Wolverhampton Wanderers 114
Woodall, William 74
Woodhall, Lucy 76
Woodhouse family 34, 76, 99, 100
Worcester diocese 7, 28, 48
Workhouse, The 45-6
World Wars 117
Wright's Lane 16, 18, 104-5, 108-10
Wyatt, Benjamin 48

Yew Tree 19

Zion's Hill 101